The wedding of Felix Reinbach and Elisa Henke
was a huge family affair typical of German weddings
in Gillespie County. Courtesy of RoShell Baker.

This beautiful volume has been made possible
thanks to the generosity of the following:

AdCasting, Inc.
KFAN/KNAF Radio

Century 21 Sunset, Realtors
Dwight & Karen Oestreich

Crenwelge Motor Sales
Crenwelge Buick-Olds
Milton M. Crenwelge

Dietzel Motel
Igler Enterprises, Inc.

Frantzen, Kaderli & Klier
Insurance Agency, Inc.

Gillespie County Historical Society, Inc.

Kwik Car Wash
Attic Mini Storage
Sam & Nancy Golden

John D. & Karen G. Haebig

Robert & Barbara Heinen

Hill Country Refrigeration

Wilbert & Clara Ann Ottmers

Sharon Joseph, Investment Broker

Judy's Liquor
Judy Vordenbaum

Knopp-Metzger Department Store, Inc.

Knopp Nursing Home
Knopp Retirement Center
Luckenbach Retirement Apts.

H. W. "Bill" & Modena Marschall

Dr. and Mrs. J. Hardin Perry

Schaetter's Funeral Home
Since 1882

The Showcase Antiques Shop
Ron & Jane Woellhof

Stroeher & Son, Inc.
Stroeher & Olfers, Inc.

Vogel Orchard, Stonewall
George & Nelda Vogel

Proceeds from its sale will be used to benefit programs
of the Gillespie County Historical Society.

Gillespie County
A View of Its Past

by Monty and Michelle Mohon

THE
DONNING COMPANY
PUBLISHERS

Copyright 1996 © by Gillespie County Historical Society

All rights reserved, including the right to reproduce this work in any form whatsoever without permission in writing from the publisher, except for brief passages in connection with a review. For information, write:

The Donning Company/Publishers
184 Business Park Drive, Suite 106
Virginia Beach, VA 23462

Barbara A. Bolton, Project Director
Tracey Emmons-Schneider, Director of Research
Elizabeth B. Bobbitt, Executive Editor
Mary E. Apperson, Graphic Designer
Dawn Kofroth, Production Manager
Tony Lillis, Director of Marketing

Library of Congress Cataloging-in-Publication Data

Mohon, Monty D., 1966–
    Gillespie County, a view of its past / by Monty D. Mohon and Michelle R. Mohon.
      p. cm.
    Includes bibliographical references (p.) and index.
    ISBN 0-89865-964-7 (hardcover : alk. paper)
    1. Gillespie County (Tex.)—History.   I. Mohon, Michelle R., 1967– . II. Title
F392.G5M64   1996
976.4'65—dc20
                                                                   95-53791
                                                                      CIP

Printed in the United States of America

HALTOM CITY PUBLIC LIBRARY

Contents

Preface	6
Chapter 1 **From Germany to Texas**	9
Chapter 2 **People of Faith**	29
Chapter 3 **The County's Architecture**	45
Chapter 4 **Improving the Land**	67
Chapter 5 **Social Life in the County**	87
Chapter 6 **Modes of Transportation**	113
Chapter 7 **The Three R's**	125
Chapter 8 **Those of Influence**	149
Chapter 9 **Fairs, Festivals, and Celebrations**	159
Chapter 10 **Trade and Commerce**	173
Bibliography	188
Index	190

Preface

The Gillespie County Historical Society (GCHS) was chartered in 1936 with the purpose of rebuilding the Vereins Kirche, the pioneer town's first general purpose structure, used for town meetings, religious meetings, a school, and store. The Society has actively continued, gaining several new properties and sponsoring many activities. As of 1995 the Historical Society's real estate holdings include the Vereins Kirche and Archives, Cross Mountain, Pioneer Home and Store, Old Methodist Church, Fassel House, Weber Sunday House, an 1800s Log Cabin, Schandua House, and many fine collections displayed within our properties.

In 1960 and 1974, the Historical Society published *Pioneers in God's Hills* and *Pioneers in God's Hills, Vol II*. These books contain primarily family histories and pictures. Both have proven to be valuable resources; and we feel *Gillespie County, A View of Its Past*, will likewise be a memorable addition to one's library. *Gillespie County, A View of Its Past* records visual memories of the last 150 years in the county. It is a reflection of the courageous character of the pioneers who settled this wilderness and built a solid foundation for our county. Likewise, the book reflects the spirit and character of the first pioneer's descendants who have continued to build on that foundation.

We wish to thank those who responded to our requests for photographs to be preserved in this book. We give special thanks to the *Fredericksburg Standard Radio Post* for its cooperation and numerous contributions. Many contributors identified everyone in their photos. We regret, however, that space constrictions made it impossible to print all the names, and for that matter all of the contributed photographs.

We also want to thank our authors, Monty and Michelle Mohon, for their many hours of hard work assembling this magnificent collection of information and photographs. They have worked diligently to produce a valuable and enjoyable book.

The book's cover painting was designed and donated by local artist John Austin Hanna. We truly appreciate this special painting depicting the early days of the pioneers—and at no cost to us.

Finally, we thank the underwriters and sponsors whose financial backing made this endeavor possible. Profits on the sale of this book will go toward maintaining our collections and our properties. We hope you enjoy the volume and the memories it evokes of the founders of this unique county and its county seat—Fredericksburg.

Sincerely,

Judy Vordenbaum, President

The Gillespie County Historical Society
Board of Directors 1995

Judy Vordenbaum, President
John Haebig, 1st Vice President
Barry Kaiser, 2nd Vice President
Sharon Joseph, Treasurer
Darlene Stehle, Secretary
Dorothy Basse
Reuben Bohnert
Mickey Crenwelge
Peggy Ernst
Jere Fuller
Dr. J. Hardin Perry
Wilbur Pressler
Jim Strackbein
George Vogel
Marcella Weiershausen

Chapter One

From Germany to Texas

The lure of the rugged, vast land of Texas was too strong for many Germans to resist. Glowing reports about Texas, a place where dreams could be attained, enticed men from all walks of life to leave their country and begin anew in America. The call was even greater in that it was coupled with a sense of uneasiness about the growing problems in the motherland.

After Texas gained its independence from Mexico, Germany was flooded with even more literature regarding the vast Republic. The German people heard the siren song from the west and indeed it captured the imagination. And why not? One author said, Texas was a place "where nails grew overnight into horseshoes." Pamphlets, books, and personal accounts were eagerly passed among a people ready for change.

By the 1840s thousands of Germans had already headed for the New World. Meanwhile, in drawing rooms across Germany, the nobility and educated were discussing the political and social unrest in Germany and the possibility of emigration. Through these meetings, Count Castell, an officer in the Austrian garrison in the Federal fortress at Mainz, initiated the idea to form a society to help German citizens emigrate to the new land. The organization, which was founded in 1842 by princes and noblemen, came to be known as the *Adelsverein* or the Society of Noblemen.

Historians have speculated on the founders' motivation for establishing the Adelsverein and have discovered no concrete explanation. Regardless of their intent, the idealistic noblemen were ill-prepared for the daunting task at hand. In their zeal

Called "Red Sun" by the Indians, John O. Meusebach was a leader. He received a fine education and spoke several languages. Although he was not one of the founding members of the Adelsverein, once he became involved he was an invaluable asset. Later Meusebach showed even greater strength of character when he led a group into the hunting grounds of the fierce Comanche to gain peace. Then Meusebach, whose motto became "Texas Forever," further served his community, this time in the state senate in 1851. Later he founded Loyal Valley. In 1936 the state erected a marker to honor the memory of this very noble man. Courtesy of Bill Marschall.

While John O. Meusebach was intent on making the new German settlements prosper, he was also awaiting a time when he could return to Germany to marry the girl on whom his heart was set. In a sad twist of events, she died shortly before the long awaited marriage was to occur. Later, to his delight, he met a young lady named Agnes Coreth. Although she was only seventeen and he was forty years old, the two had much in common and were married in New Braunfels. Their marriage was blessed with eleven children. Pictured center is Agnes Coreth, behind her from left to right are her daughter, Antonio Meusebach Marschall, Helen Marschall Altgelt, and on her lap Esther Altgelt, Helen Marschall Altgelt's daughter. Courtesy of Bill Marschall.

they bought a worthless land grant from a Frenchman named Bourgeois, who posed as a nobleman. After determining that he was an impostor and the grant was fraudulent, they resumed their quest. The need for land was urgent because the Society had already advertised opportunities to emigrate, and fellow countrymen were preparing to set sail for the new world.

In the midst of their search for land, one of the Adelsverein noblemen, Prince Carl Solms, a first cousin to Queen Victoria of England, met an American named Henry Fisher. Fisher had arrived in Bremen, Germany, as the official consul for the Republic of Texas, giving him the appearance of credibility in the eyes of the prince. Thus, when Fisher described a grant which contained four million acres of fine farm land, Prince Solms did not question Fisher's integrity. In truth, Henry Fisher had never laid eyes on the land. Furthermore, the grant was located in the heart of Comanche country.

With Prince Solms' recommendation, the Adelsverein purchased land from Fisher. That purchase came to be known as the Fisher-Miller grant. They had lost money and time with the first land deal, but the Noblemen were undeterred. The Adelsverein made adjustments in their advertising campaign and described the Fisher-Miller grant as "fertile and healthy lands."

Immigrants were on their way but there was a snag in the Adelsverein's master plan. A condition of the grant required the land be surveyed *before* it could be occupied. Once surveyed, each settler would receive 640 acres if he were married and 320 acres if he were single. Fisher, the self proclaimed "expert," told the Adelsverein that eighty thousand American dollars could place the settlers on the land and pay for a few months' provisions. Historians estimate that it probably would have cost eighty thousand dollars just to have the land surveyed, consequently leaving the society with a grave shortage of funds to settle hundreds of Germans in Texas.

In November and December 1844, three ships with about seven hundred settlers arrived in Galveston. They made their way to Carlshafen, now known as Indianola, where the only facilities existing were a few crude buildings and a warehouse. The weary travelers camped in tents on the wet beach for two months. Because the land grant had not yet been surveyed, there was no place for the settlers to go. Prince Solms was finally able to purchase a thirteen-hundred-acre tract of land for eight hundred dollars along the intersection of the Comal and Guadalupe Rivers. On Monday, March 10, 1845, the Prince and this first group of settlers began the trek toward their land.

The original emigration papers issued had a general description of each settler. The papers contained no photograph, but a written description was given of the physical characteristics, i.e. Nose: long, Face: round, Hair: brown. Courtesy of John and Dorothea Cotter.

On March 21st, the first colonists reached the site of present day New Braunfels. There they received a land allocation at no cost to them, since they were not able to acquire their land within the still unsurveyed Fisher-Miller Grant. As planned, the settlers were given a daily ration of meat, corn, flour, salt, rice, beans, bacon, etc. Prince Solms wrote of the trip, "Thus I had completed my assignment, but not without privation, hardship, and many dangers. However, I endured as is becoming a German gentleman and attribute it, first of all, to the protection of the Highest . . ." (Penniger, p. 22)

These first settlers fared well. Unfortunately, the next group encountered more difficulties. The Adelsverein had grossly underestimated the cost of their venture, based on Fisher's advice, and had also made unplanned expenditures, such as

For many years, children must have been enthralled by the stories the men told of their encounter with the Indians. Meusebach's rendition of the day made such a vivid impression on his children, that his daughter was able to paint it. This painting has come to symbolize the essence of the treaty and the end of the struggle between the Indians and the settlers. It serves also as a tribute to Meusebach whose bravery benefited not only his own children, but all the children of Gillespie County. Courtesy of the *Standard*.

the New Braunfels tract of land. Now the Society was perilously close to financial disaster. Prince Solms secured more financing, but the loans reached such great amounts that he was forced to retire from his position with the Adelsverein.

On February 24, 1845, the Society of Noblemen appointed John O. Meusebach to take over the administrative position of the Society, which included the formidable task of organizing the Society's finances. Upon analysis, Meusebach realized they were twenty thousand dollars in debt. Adding to the Adelsverein's insolvency, all of the settlers who had made it to New Braunfels had made cash deposits to the Society which were to be returned to them. And over four thousand new immigrants were due to arrive.

Meusebach gave the directors the bleak financial report and solicited more funds. He then began procuring another tract of land to accommodate the new colonists until they could claim their land within the Fisher-Miller grant. In August of 1845, Meusebach headed west. He found ten thousand acres with good soil about eighty miles west of New Braunfels. He bought

On December 5, 1848, welcome relief came to the struggling colony in the form of Fort Martin Scott. Old settlers remembered when, as children, they gathered grains left over by the soldiers' horses to take home to their mothers who then washed and ground the grain for meal.

Fort Martin Scott was abandoned on December 29, 1853, after Fort Mason was established. The fort was again occupied during the Civil War by the Confederates from 1861 to 1865. It was militarily occupied for the last time for three months by the United States Cavalry ending December 28, 1866.

After that, the buildings that once were home to soldiers were occupied by a variety of people. Several families made temporary homes within the fort, which was gradually torn down by individuals who perhaps needed building supplies for their own pursuits.

In 1872 J. W. Braeutigam purchased the remains of the old fort. At that time only two buildings were in good repair. Braeutigam erected a saloon and built the first dance hall in the area. Fairs and horse racing (the only horse racing in this part of the state of Texas) were also held on his property. Apparently, large sums of money often passed hands and this perhaps was the motivation for the robbery and murder of J. W. Braeutigam on the night of September 10, 1884. One of the men implicated in the murder, William Allison, lost his life a year later when a fire broke out at the county jail.

The property is now owned by the city of Fredericksburg and serves as a backdrop for reenactments of military activities. This painting by G. G. H. Lentz shows the layout of Fort Martin Scott as based on sketches and descriptions given in military records of the National Archives. Used with permission of G. G. H. Lentz.

The Reverend Heinrich Wilhelm Basse and his wife, Fredericke Charlotte, left his pastorate of fourteen years and entered a journey that proved to be dramatically life-changing for the family. They arrived in Fredericksburg in the Fall of 1846 with some of the members from his church in Germany. Basse soon began making efforts to organize a Protestant church and later in 1847, participated in the ceremony to dedicate the newly constructed Vereins Kirche. Times proved to be hard for the pastor as he saw his family suffer great hardship. Torn between the desire to serve in the ministry and the call to fulfill his biblical responsibility to provide for his family, Pastor Basse turned over his flock to Reverend B. Dangers three years after the church's inception, and went into the mercantile business. He still continued to be called "Pastor Basse" and often served as counselor and friend to the fledgling community. Courtesy of Dr. and Mrs. Adolph Basse.

the land on credit and returned to New Braunfels by the end of October.

When Meusebach returned he organized a group of thirty-six men to return to the new land to lay out a wagon road and to conduct surveys. This journey was reported in the *Democratic Telegraph and Texas Register*. "We learn that Capt. Murchison [one of the thirty-six] had lately made an expedition with a party of the German emigrants of New Braunfels to the valley of the Pedernales . . . The persons who have visited this valley speak of it in glowing terms and consider it one of the most fertile, healthy and beautiful sections of the West." (German Settlers in Texas, p. 150)

Around November 1, 1845, Meusebach received word that 4,304 immigrants were departing from Germany and that credit of twenty-four thousand dollars was available in New Orleans. Unfortunately, this amount was not enough to provide for the certain influx of new immigrants and the Society was now even further in debt. Meusebach estimated he needed approximately $140,000, an extraordinary amount of money at that time. Still he handled the situation with aplomb and made it his goal to secure some type of financing in order to get them through this hopeless situation.

Meusebach traveled to Galveston to meet the settlers and to provide temporary shelter for them. He had hired teamsters to transport the settlers to New Braunfels. About half of the Germans had arrived at the safe haven of New Braunfels when the Mexican-American War began. Unfortunately, the teamsters quickly abandoned their post with Meusebach and sought more lucrative jobs with the military. Rather than wait on the beach for transportation, some five hundred young German men joined the United States Army. The remaining two thousand settlers were left at Carlshafen. Some attempted to walk to New Braunfels while others waited hopefully on the beach in the middle of an exceedingly rainy winter. Many of the settlers dug caves in the ground to escape the elements. Soon disease broke out and hundreds of settlers, including children, died before ever reaching New Braunfels. Making matters worse still, a scurvy-type disease broke out claiming hundreds, perhaps thousands, of lives.

Rumors regarding the financial status of the Society also began spreading and many of the settlers grew angry and discontent. Morale was very low, indeed. "While the scurvy epidemic was at its height, men and women became bereft of reason, family ties were broken, and the wretched people tried to forget their misery by dancing, carousing and drinking."

Meusebach, observing the hopelessness of the situation, determined "all newly arrived colonists [should be] transported

Friedrich (Fritz) Lochte along with his parents were on the first wagon train to Fredericksburg. Photo taken during the 1890s. Courtesy of RoShell Baker.

Heinrich Frederick Welge was one of several hearty pioneers who, rather than wait for transportation to be provided in Indianola, walked 165 miles from the shores of the Gulf of Mexico to New Braunfels. Once he arrived in New Braunfels, he rested and then like many others, proceeded on to Fredericksburg. Welge eventually settled in Cherry Springs and owned a nine-thousand-acre ranch. Almost two-thirds of the ranch is still in the family's possession. Courtesy of Laura Welge Evers.

as soon as possible to Fredericksburg, since it was considered to be the most healthy location." (Penniger, p. 24)

Meanwhile, Meusebach, still under duress about the financial condition of the Society, realized the only way to acquire the financial assistance needed was to alert the German newspapers. Once the Germans were informed of the severe hardship their countrymen were being forced to endure in the new land, they demanded an explanation from the Adelsverein. This pressure proved to be the proper motivation, and at long last sixty thousand dollars was received by the struggling colonization effort.

The first group of settlers sent to Fredericksburg left New Braunfels on April 24, 1846. Approximately 120 men, women, and children along with the Society's soldiers, were in the ox cart wagon train.

Hermann Lungkwitz, his new bride Elizabeth, his mother, brother, and bride's family, all set sail for the New World full of eager anticipation. Completely untrained for the farmer's way of life the group left fine, fancy things behind and boarded a rocking ship headed for Hoboken, New Jersey. Their final destination proved to be the Live Oak community near Fredericksburg, Texas. There they found friendship in Carl Guenther, founder of Pioneer Mills, and many others who had been brought up in a much more refined way than they now were living. His wife, Elizabeth, learned to milk cows and work hard as a pioneer woman. Lungkwitz, his brother Adolph, and brother-in-law, Richard Petri, toiled together to eke out an existence from the land.

In his spare time, Lungkwitz painted. This lithograph depicts Fredericksburg in the early days. His paintings focused on the landscape of the surrounding area. After living in Fredericksburg for a season, he moved to San Antonio where he attempted to make a living as a photographer. In later years, after the death of his beloved wife Elizabeth, he often traveled back to Fredericksburg to visit his brother, Adolph, and to continue sketching the hills and trees of his home in America—Fredericksburg. "Friedrichsburg" toned lithograph (hand colored) 1859; Amon Carter Museum, Ft. Worth, Texas.

In the early pioneering days sickness was common; a new climate, intense, hard labor, and poor diet were all contributors. Fortunately, the new Fredericksburg community had the faithful Dr. Christian Althaus. After being trained as a medic in the Prussian Army Medical Corps, he arrived in Fredericksburg. His primary "territory" was the Rheingold, Cave Creek area. Dr. Althaus made his own medicine from herbs, seeds, roots, plants, and tree bark that he pounded into powder. His treatment for diphtheria was so successful that he was employed by the U.S. Government to go to Bandera and surrounding areas to treat those afflicted with the disease.

Dr. Althaus was an ingenious and inventive man. He had the first house in Gillespie County, perhaps even in Texas, with running water. He built the house around a flowing spring and thus had running water. He lined the walls around the spring with shelves and then kept milk, butter, and fresh meat on the shelves in order to keep them cool.

He was also skilled in more than one task. He helped with the construction of the Vereins Kirche, served as a government agent, as a freighter at Fort Martin Scott, had a workshop making saddles and riding gear, served for three years as a county commissioner, and raised seven children with his wife, Anna Marie Behrens. Courtesy of Ella Mae Herber.

The first doctor in the new settlement was Dr. Schubert. Schubert was recommended for his position by Henry Fisher. Unfortunately for the settlers who had placed their trust in the Adelsverein, Dr. Schubert did not have the best interest of the colony at heart, often using his position of authority unscrupulously. Later it was discovered that the name Schubert was actually an alias, his real name being Strubach. Meusebach soon replaced him with Dr. Wilhelm Keidel (pictured), a recent graduate of George Augustus University Medical School in Germany. He had arrived in America in 1845 and served in the military as a private surgeon while Texas sought to gain its independence. Meusebach persuaded Keidel to come to Fredericksburg. He served the county faithfully and treated the Indians in exchange for turkey or venison. He was chosen as the county's first chief justice and was a trustee at the Live Oak School. Dr. Wilhelm Keidel's son and grandsons went on to practice medicine, dentistry, and pharmacy in the county, continuing the family tradition. Courtesy of Mrs. J. Hardin Perry.

The sixteen day trip was not without adventure. In places, the way was so swampy that the sojourners had to gather rocks to build the road and dam up water. Also they encountered a band of Delaware Indians who appeared to be friendly. But, when the wagon train crossed a small creek, both a gunshot and a cry for help were heard. All expected the worst, but fears were quickly put at bay. John Schmidt, one of the Society's soldiers, had simply shot a bear. Later that same day, Society trooper Conrad Merz killed a panther.

Friday evening, May 8, 1846, the immigrants arrived at the sight of their new home: raw wilderness. The group spent the night under the live oak trees and dined on the kill of the day, bear and panther meat. It was reported that one of the ladies, Mrs. Lochte, delighted the group by eating the head of the bear and declaring it very tasty.

That summer, a second wagon train arrived. Those among the second train were greeted by the sight of the labors of the first group. They had built a stockade for shelter and tilled a garden. The land was soon divided into tracts. Because of its dark, rich soil, and the proximity to water, most of the residents desired the tracts on what is now Creek Street in Fredericksburg. The settlers began making homes and planting gardens, but the intent was still to move to their land on the Fisher-Miller grant.

The settlers struggled and food was scarce. Their poor diet caused a disease thought to be similar to dysentery, which killed many of the newcomers. The death toll was so high that the two-wheeled oxcart made its journey back and forth to the cemetery almost all day without stopping. One colonist, Mr. B. Blum, wrote, "No pen can describe the heartache and despair which the helpless survivors suffered." (Penniger, p. 36).

In the meantime, Meusebach made plans to have the Fisher-Miller grant surveyed so that the immigrants could finally receive the land promised to them. The terms of the grant stipulated that the land had to be occupied and surveyed by the fall of 1847. John James, district surveyor, stated that he and his men would not go further into the grant until a treaty had been made with the Indians. Time was running out and although confrontation with the Comanches seemed inevitable, Meusebach felt the colonization must proceed. Thus, he made preparations to meet with the Indians.

To Meusebach, proving that the Indian territory could be penetrated successfully was important not only for the colonization effort, but also for the morale of the colonists. With that in mind, forty men were prepared for this mission by January 22, 1847. The company included German settlers,

American surveyors, and five Mexicans. One of the group, Lorenzo de Rozas, had been kidnapped as a child by the Comanches. He served as Meusebach's guide and interpreter.

The long trip was not without calamity. While on a buffalo hunt, a gun belonging to one of their most able men exploded, wounding the man and sending him back home. Shortly thereafter, the camp's fire ignited a brush fire that the men fought for thirty-six hours.

In spite of a faltering start, the men proceeded onward. While on the trek the group had the good fortune to meet with a friendly Shawnee Indian. After sharing their supper with him they discovered the Shawnee was traveling with six to eight other Indians. Meusebach, knowing how difficult it was for the white man to have a successful hunt in that vicinity, employed three of the Shawnee to accompany them as hunters.

Now the pursuers of peace were in Indian territory and the Shawnees assured them that reconnaissance Comanches had spotted them and were carefully monitoring their progress, putting the pioneers on guard.

Groups of four men were on constant watch for periods of two hours each. Since all of our watches failed us we were compelled to estimate the time periods. It usually happened that daylight came two hours late. That is, the last watch had to serve four hours instead of two.

While standing watch at night after a day's travel was tedious, it also proved interesting to observe our associates and to note how the mixture of many nationalities dressed in their respective costumes was reflected by the huge fires against the dark background. We shared Baron Von Meusebach's fire, which was in the center of the camp. After the evening meal he would frequently hold us captive with his cheerful mood and

Left: Emil Kriewitz was an interesting figure in the early years of Fredericksburg. He joined the military after arriving in Indianola, in part because of inadequate transportation to New Braunfels. He and several others were commissioned by the military to aid Meusebach in his effort to gain peace with the Comanches. After the peace treaty was solidified, he lived with the Indians fulfilling one of the stipulations of the peace treaty as an "Indian Ambassador." Part of being an "Indian Ambassador" involved living with the Indians in order to understand them. According to Kriewitz, "several of the candidates for the office of Indian agent withdrew when the time came for the appointment. [I] decided to risk [my] 'scalp,' because the safety of the proposed colonies depended on the friendliest possible relations with the Indians."(Penniger, p. 49) Later Kriewitz guided the groups to Bettina, Leiningen, and Castell. Photo Courtesy of Vicki Swanson.

Jacob Kuechler came to Texas in 1847 and participated in an intriguing experiment attempted by the Germans. The goal was to form a communistic utopia within the land grant. Meusebach chose a site on the Llano River. The group of utopian colonizers were known as the "forty." The "forty," all educated young men, landed in Galveston. Emil Kriewitz, who had lived with the Indians, served as the group's guide. The colony was named Bettina for Bettina von Arnim who was a writer, a well known intellectual, and a personal friend of Meusebach. The experiment did not last long as many of the new settlers found that they would rather live by the dictum "Ede, bibe, post mortem nulla voluptas" (Eat and drink for after death there is no joy), rather than carrying their share of the work load. Many of the "forty" then moved to the Comfort or Sisterdale area. Kuechler moved to Fredericksburg and became the county surveyor for Gillespie County. He later married Richard Petri's sister, Marie, and lived in the Live Oak community until the Civil War. This portrait of Kuechler was sketched by his brother-in-law, Petri. Used with permission from the Texas Memorial Museum.

It was a life of luxury and sophistication that many of the new settlers left behind to begin a new way of life. For these men and women, life in Germany must have paled in comparison to the danger, excitement, and violence that they soon faced in the large land of Texas. William Friederich Eduard Klier was such a person. The son of wealthy, educated parents, he left Germany in 1849, when he was but a mere fourteen years old, in order to avoid three years of compulsory military training.

He arrived in Fredericksburg ready for adventure. Young William and a partner carried mail on mules from Fort Martin Scott to Forts Mason, McKavett, San Saba, and Concho during a time when the Indians posed a great danger. After his postal adventures, William worked alongside Jacob Kuechler as a surveyor in the 1850s.

When the Civil War began, Klier, like most of the community, supported the Union. Through his support of the Union, Klier found himself involved in the Nueces Massacre which he was fortunate to survive and escape to his home. Unfortunately, his presence was discovered. He was captured and taken to a camp near Boerne, where if it weren't for the intercession of a comrade, he would have been hung. Klier was then relocated to a prison camp on the Gulf Coast where he remained for the rest of the war. Later, he returned to Fredericksburg and farmed for the rest of his days. Photo courtesy of Alton Klier.

conversation until late into the night. The Mexicans, as a rule, slept near. [They], like all their countrymen, were strongly devoted to the game of monte (a card game). Their lively manners stood in sharp contrast with the peaceful behavior of our Shawnees who lay speechless about the fire and smoked their sumac. The latter is a dried leaf of a common Texas shrub. Only at midnight did they let their melancholy songs resound. Another group included the Americans who grouped themselves with the Society troopers. It was a colorful assembly. (Penniger, p. 38-39)

At long last de Rozas was given an audience with the Comanches. After negotiations between de Rozas and a Comanche chief, the parties agreed that Meusebach and his men could meet with the tribesmen. On February 7, 1847, the group was met by a large band of Indians all dressed in colorful attire. "Now we were in a somewhat precarious situation, because our small band of forty men found itself right in the midst of five or six thousand Indians, especially a tribe which because of the desire for plunder and preference for white scalps had caused such widespread fear . . . " (Penniger, p. 40) The Indians let de Rozas know that they desired only four or five of the group to come closer. When the five courageous pioneers got within one hundred paces of the five or six thousand Indians, de Rozas told the small group that if they

Left: Richard Petri came to Texas with his brother-in-law and fellow artist, Hermann Lungkwitz, in 1952. The two studied art together at one of the most renowned art schools in all of Europe located in Dresden.

Petri battled with his health in Germany, but the sea air and the journey to the new land proved invigorating. Once they reached their destination in Fredericksburg, hard work and toil faced the young artists. The two, along with Lungkwitz's brother Adolph, made a fine go of it and managed to continue sketching when the rugged pioneer life permitted.

Petri was fascinated with the Indians and spent many hours sketching them. His niece and nephew, Max and Martha, were also favorite studies. The two artists' talent was a welcome asset to the community and the men were called upon on numerous occasions to paint backdrops or posters for different festivals and productions.

Unfortunately, Petri still struggled with his health. After only a few years of living in Gillespie County he became extremely sick with fever. He awoke in the night and wandered down to the Pedernales River on which their property was located. In a delirium he stumbled into the river and drowned. Although he spent but a short time in the United States, his drawings left a priceless legacy.

would fire their guns, the Indians would look upon them favorably and think them brave. They did so, and the Comanches responded in kind.

The men were invited to spend the night in the Indians' camp, but they gracefully declined and made a camp across the stream only to be joined by a different Comanche tribe which was passing through the area. When the men prepared their meals the Indians crowded in "with such a ravenous hunger that we could scarcely satisfy our own hunger."

On February 9, 1847, several horsemen dressed in European attire surprised the men by riding into their camp. It was Major Neighbors, the Indian agent of Texas, and Delaware Chief Jim Shaw. They had been sent by the governor of Texas to warn Meusebach against approaching the Indians. But Meusebach refused to be dissuaded from his mission.

Meusebach then informed the Comanches of his intentions to travel to the old Spanish Fort known as San Saba before returning for their agreed upon meeting. Because supplies were low, the group divided with some of the men returning to Fredericksburg.

Meusebach's group reached the fort at San Saba with no trouble from the Indians. Meusebach and his friend, Dr. Ferdinand Roemer, a naturalist and geologist, collected minerals and fossils. The group then began making its way back for the meeting with the Comanches.

Soon they reached an Indian tribe under the command of Chief Mopechucope, (or old owl). The next morning Meusebach and his men watched twenty warriors make their way out of the camp as they headed toward Mexico on a raiding party. Later that same day, the chiefs assembled. Buffalo hides were placed around a fire, which was lit for the purpose of lighting the peace pipe. Meusebach began his remarks, with Jim Shaw as an interpreter. "I have come a great distance to see you and to smoke the peace pipe with you . . . "

The words of Meusebach were met with favor by the Indians and a peace treaty was formed. Meusebach had accomplished a remarkable feat. After celebrations the Fredericksburg group returned home much to the relief of the townspeople.

Part of the treaty involved the hospitality of the Fredericksburg community. Various sources claim that the Indians eagerly took advantage of the town's graciousness by visiting often. Sometimes Indians went so far as to enter settlers' homes unannounced. The peace treaty was never broken by either side, although an occasional marauding band of Indians would reign terror on the Fredericksburg community.

In 1870 the Lehmann family in Loyal Valley fell victim to a band of roving Apaches. The Lehmann children had been sent to the field to scare away birds when the Indians kidnapped Hermann Lehmann and his younger brother, Willie. Once captured, the boys were stripped, placed on horses and generally mistreated as they road naked in the blasting hot Texas sun. The younger brother was knocked off his horse and left behind. Fortunately he made his way to a road where a stranger found him and saw to it that he was returned to his home.

Hermann, on the other hand, remained in captivity for the next nine years. During that time he endured harsh treatment, experienced brushes with death and witnessed countless heinous acts. Interestingly, at one point the Indians with whom he was traveling met with another group of Indians who also had a German boy captive. The two were able to discuss their plight together in German—a welcome relief for Lehmann. Unfortunately, the next morning the band of Indians was gone, leaving him alone once more. The Apaches told him that his family was dead and in due time the young boy became thoroughly "Indianized" even participating in the violent raiding parties. Later he killed the tribe's medicine man in a late night, drunken brawl. Because the other Apaches would avenge the death by killing Lehmann, he became an exile.

After a year of solitude he encountered a group of Comanches, and in an act of loneliness and determination, boldly asked if he could join them. They consented—a great relief to Lehmann who seemingly was an enemy to all of mankind. After a few years of living with the Comanches, the government placed final pressures on the Indians to move onto the reservations. Simultaneously, military measures were taken to remove all white prisoners from the Indians' ranks and return them to their families. Hermann Lehmann eluded such attempts and was adopted by the Comanche chief, Quanah Parker. Eventually, Lehmann reluctantly conceded and returned to his family in Loyal Valley. Through the efforts of his younger brother Willie, Hermann was able to adapt to his people once again. Courtesy of Esther Lehmann.

Although the Indians proved to be a formidable danger when the settlers first arrived following the peace treaty, the settlers and the Comanches enjoyed a peaceful relationship. The Indians visited the town frequently and traded honey, meat, hides and other goods with local merchants and the soldiers at Fort Martin Scott. This season of peace continued until the outbreak of the Civil War when some of the Indians became, once again, highly hostile to the settlers throughout the area. It was during this time that Indians quietly approached Richard Petri's home. The Indians were spotted and the women and children were quickly ushered inside the house. On a hunch Petri grabbed his sketching material and remained on the porch sketching the approaching Indians. His impulse was correct. The Indians were amicable and fascinated with Petri's artistic rendition of them. The artist's fascination with Indians continued and he was said to have sorely missed them when the Indians became relegated to reservations. Many of his works centered around the life of the Indians. Used with permission from Texas Memorial Museum.

This building was the first Gillespie County Courthouse. It was constructed in 1855 and replaced in 1882 by the building now known as Pioneer Memorial Library. The building was razed in 1940 to make way for the United States Post office located on the corner of Main Street and Crockett in Fredericksburg. Courtesy of the *Standard*.

In 1848 welcome relief came to the settlement in the form of United States soldiers. Fort Martin Scott was built west of Fredericksburg giving the settlement more security from the Indians. Furthermore, the soldiers' need for services and hard goods gave the community the economic boost it so badly needed. The soldiers needed everything from seeds, to hair tonic, to bear oil. Their most pressing "need" was brandy and whiskey from the store across the street from the famous Nimitz Hotel which may account for the amount of trouble they also brought into the town.

That same year the town of Fredericksburg began making efforts to withdraw from the massive Bexar County and form its own smaller county. On February 23, 1848, the county was conceived and given the name Gillespie County in honor of Captain Robert A. Gillespie who was killed in action in the war with Mexico. Fredericksburg was designated as the county seat. The new county encompassed portions of what was formerly Bexar and Travis Counties and initially contained parts of what is today Blanco, Llano, and Mason Counties.

The county had no courthouse, and official county meetings were conducted in the home of the first chief justice, Dr. William Keidel. Meusebach had employed Dr. Keidel to replace Dr. Schubert as the Adelsverein physician. County Clerk John M. Hunter safeguarded the records of these meetings in his store until 1850. Unfortunately, after Hunter killed an unruly soldier from Fort Martin Scott, the soldier's friends sought revenge and burned Hunter's store to the ground.

In 1849 Fredericksburg received the blessing of being the last town on Upper Immigrant Road until El Paso. The forty-niners stopped in Fredericksburg for supplies before continuing their quest west for gold. This blessing came with a curse—cholera. During those hard times, Indians repaid the hospitality paid to them. Chief Santana himself brought food to settlers frequently and the community felt much remorse when they heard he too had succumbed to cholera.

Once the Fisher-Miller grant was surveyed, the colonization effort continued. Five colonies were formed before the Adelsverein folded. One of those, Castell, Texas, is still in existence. The others soon dwindled to nothing. In an ironic twist the temporary settlements of New Braunfels and Fredericksburg continued to thrive.

Members of Holy Ghost Lutheran celebrate the birth of Christ through a nativity scene. Note the German "Peace on Earth good will toward men." wording on the banner. Photo Courtesy of Holy Ghost Lutheran Church.

Chapter Two

People of Faith

"It is many weeks since I left your house . . . Many an hour on the sea voyage was shortened for me in recalling the love and affection each one of you bestowed upon me. In the evenings when I walked alone on deck and admired the beautiful sky, moon and stars and watched the billowing ocean, I felt very close to you in spirit. It is impossible to express the feeling which comes over you when walking on deck at night. You are amazed at the power of Almighty God. No other place can give you so good an opportunity for examining your own soul."
   —Carl Hilmar Guenther, a Gillespie County colonist

Leaving friends, family, and often personal wealth behind, many Germans arrived in Fredericksburg only to face the death of a spouse, a child, or both. For many of the first settlers, only their faith in God enabled them to endure the confounding problems they encountered in this new land.

The first immigrants were primarily Evangelisch, now known as Protestant Lutherans. However, there were also a number of intellectuals, or *Freethinkers*, who dismissed the concept of God and made disbelief, rather than belief, their credo.

Regardless of each settler's personal outlook on religious matters, the Adelsverein required each settler to have a certificate of baptism to be accepted for immigration. In turn the Adelsverein pledged to provide a church for each new colony. The first organized Christian church services were held in November 1846 under an oak tree south of the first courthouse. Reverend Heinrich S. W. Basse, hired by the Adelsverein to

The Vereins Kirche was dedicated May 9, 1847. Indians joined the celebration alongside the colonists. This sketch titled, "The Church at Fredericksburg, Texas - 70 Miles North of San Antonio" was done on January 24, 1849, by Seth Eastman. Eastman's stint with the military enabled him to capture much of the hill country in Texas prior to the widespread use of photography. Used with permission from the McNay Art Museum through a gift from the Pearl Brewing Company.

serve as the community pastor, conducted the services. The new arrivals continued to meet under that same tree for nearly one year until they built a permanent structure.

Meanwhile, the Society's notorious Dr. Schubert designed Fredericksburg's first church building. Named the *Vereins Kirche* (Society Church), or the *Kaffeemuehle* due to its resemblance of a coffee mill, the octagonal building was constructed with the best *fachwerk* material available and built with defense in mind. Strategically placed windows enabled the settlers to keep watch on all sides and defend their little hamlet if the need arose. A cannon was placed near the Vereins Kirche and used to signal impending danger. The building had two doors, one for the women to enter the church and one for the men to enter. During the services men and women regularly sat on opposite sides of the building. Reverend Basse conducted the first services in the Vereins Kirche, which were Protestant in nature. These services were not agreeable to all the Fredericksburg residents and various groups splintered from the first church to form congregations more to their liking.

The first to break ranks from the Vereins Kirche congregation were the Catholics. In addition to their regular meeting with the Protestants at the Vereins Kirche, the Catholics also met at Johann Leyendecker's house for prayer and reading of the scripture. In 1848 the small group purchased a lot on the corner of Orange and San Antonio Streets for eighteen dollars, where they planned to build their own church. To assist with their building project, the members of the Protestant fellowship gave the Catholics a stipend for their monetary interest in the Vereins Kirche. The first Catholic church was a wooden structure. Later Peter Schandua supervised the construction of a larger stone church known today as the *Marienkirche*.

While Catholics established their parish, a group of six families planned to procure a Lutheran pastor. The year was 1849, and the town was overcome by the cholera epidemic. The group assigned a tailor, Friederich Wilhelm Schumacher, in whose house the group occasionally met, the task of finding a pastor. He searched diligently until he found a suitable man, Pastor Eduard Schneider. Schneider was asked not only to pastor their flock, but also to conduct regular prayer meetings aimed at alleviating the cholera epidemic. Upon his arrival he organized and lead prayer services twice daily.

After the plague abated, Schumacher and the other Lutherans had a new disappointment to face. The ardent Reverend Schneider was not a Lutheran at all, but rather a Methodist pastor. With their hopes dashed, the Lutherans resumed their search for a minister. That same year Pastor Basse's service to the Vereins Kirche fellowship ended. With exhausted resources the Adelsverein was unable to pay him. Consequently, Pastor Basse felt pressure to engage in business to better provide for

According to tradition, in 1848 John Durst discovered a cross thought to be placed on the mountain by Spanish missionaries on what is now known as Cross Mountain. Later a visiting Bohemian priest, Father Menzel, replaced the cross as a sign of civilization and redemption. Today, several crosses later, the cross shines brightly each night. The mountain was purchased by the Gillespie County Historical Society in order to preserve the mountain. This sketch of the mountain was done by Seth Eastman who captured much of the countryside in and around Fredericksburg before it became fully tamed by the settlers. This piece is titled "View from Fredericksburg, Texas" and was sketched on February 24, 1849. Used with permission from the McNay Art Museum through a gift from the Pearl Brewing Company.

It is the custom within the Lutheran Church to go through confirmation at the age of thirteen or fourteen. The Catechism was learned in the German language until the 1940s. The students memorized many songs, psalms, and scriptures, including the Apostles' Creed, the Lord's Prayer, and the Ten Commandments. This was the confirmation class of 1888. Top row from left to right are: Max Eckert, Emil Kordzik, Adolf Lochte, and Louis Hirsch. In the second row are: Maria Maner, Augusta Feller, Alice Feller, and Clara Eckert. In the third row are: Theresa Wahrmund, Pastor E. DeGeller, and Anna Kast. In the fourth row are: Ottilie Kordzik, Alfred Henke, Heinrich Sauer, and Emilie Feller. In the fifth row are: Heinrich Tatsch, Friedrich Maner, August Petermann, and Friederich Kleck. Courtesy of Holy Ghost Lutheran.

In the late 1840s six Orthodox Lutheran families withdrew from the Vereins Kirche to form their own church. In 1853 the group was able to purchase for forty-five dollars a piece of property on what is now Main Street in Fredericksburg. The proposed new church building had an estimated cost of twelve hundred dollars. Unfortunately, there was as shortage of cash at the time. The devout Lutherans compensated for this by donating supplies and their labor to build the church. By 1854 the cornerstone had been laid for the new church building. This 1884 photo is the original church after renovation work had been done. The present day Zion Lutheran Church is the same building with further additions and is the oldest church building in Fredericksburg. Courtesy of Zion Lutheran Church.

Rev. Gottlieb Burchard Dangers left Germany for Texas in 1845. By 1849 he arrived in Fredericksburg and served the community for twenty years as pastor of the community church which met in the Vereins Kirche. At various times when the need arose, he was also persuaded to serve as a teacher for the local schoolchildren. Pastor Dangers and his wife were not unfamiliar with sorrow and suffering. They had six children, three of whom died of diphtheria within five days of one another. During Danger's ministry he baptized 1,061, confirmed 525, married 187 couples, and conducted funeral services for 256 members of the community. Photo from Vereins Kirche.

his family. Although he left the post as the official pastor, townspeople still referred to him as Pastor Basse and many turned to him in their time of trial. Reverend Burchard Dangers, who had recently arrived in Fredericksburg, replaced Pastor Basse.

At long last in 1852 the group of six Lutheran families found their first pastor, Rev. Philip F. Zizelmann. Soon their numbers increased, and they wrote a church constitution for the newly named Zion Lutheran Church. Two years later in 1854 they laid the cornerstone for their building. Zion Lutheran, now the oldest church building in the county, is located on West Main where services continue to be held.

Pastor Schneider remained in Fredericksburg and in 1849, began a Methodist church. By 1855 the group built a place of worship on San Antonio Street, the first Methodist church in the county. Today the original Methodist Church building is owned by the Gillespie County Historical Society.

As new churches grew out of the Vereins Kirche, Pastor Dangers continued leading the community fellowship for twenty

Zion Lutheran celebrated the seventy-fifth anniversary of its constitutional founding in 1927. Pictured are the congregation, Pastor and Mrs. F. A. Bracher, their children, and guests. The photo was taken in front of Zion's eighty-five-foot tower which had been added during the renovation of 1908 when Pastor I. Glatzle was their pastor. Courtesy of Zion Lutheran Church.

years. Other men followed him. Under Hermann's leadership the name Evangelical Holy Ghost was adopted. Christian Koch was the next pastor and then came Pastor Heinzelmann. Heinzelmann created dissension after making changes in the way the church was operated. This controversy led another group of communicants to leave the church in 1887. The new church, Evangelical-Protestant church, is today known as Bethany Lutheran.

Still a group continued to attend worship services at the Vereins Kirche until the building no longer proved adequate. Mr. and Mrs. Carl Priess donated a city lot on San Antonio Street and the congregation built what is today Holy Ghost Lutheran church. Construction began in 1888 and in 1893 the building was dedicated. The pastor confirmed twenty-eight young Christians at the dedication ceremony.

The Vereins Kirche, the original church building in Gillespie County, was later torn down after nearly fifty years of use. The congregations which sprang from the Vereins Kirche conducted their services strictly in German as late as 1940, when the English language was gradually integrated into the meetings. Holy Ghost Lutheran continued to offer a German service until the 1980s. Over the years, a variety of denominations have become a part of the community, serving together with the county's original churches.

In 1952 the Episcopal Mission of St. Barnabas was formed by five families. Two years later St. Barnabas purchased the Walter homestead which had remained in the family since Peter Walter built his home there in 1848. The five Episcopal families met in the old Walter home for ten years. In fact, President Johnson and First Lady Lady Bird occasionally attended the little church along with their Secret Service agents and visiting dignitaries. By 1964 the church had outgrown the sturdy, old edifice and they built a larger place of worship. Today the quaint Walter home serves as a chapel. The well that once was the Walters' source for water is today in use as a sign. One of the grapevines in the garden area, said to have been brought from Germany by Peter Walter, still bears grapes each year. The lady seated in the photograph is thought to be his granddaughter, Minna Walters. Courtesy of Bessie Evers.

Holy Ghost Lutheran Church members and their friends gather to celebrate the first confirmation in the church building which was begun in 1888. The church was completed in 1893. Note the penciled tower that was still under construction. Courtesy of Mrs. Guenther Pfeister.

Holy Ghost Lutheran's Confirmation Class of 1901 sitting in front of the church. Seated from right to left are: Augusta Hahne, Manuela Kleck, Meta Kramer, Minna Kramer, Cora Moellering, Erna Pfiester, Alma Priess, Alice Priess, Meta Ransleben, Lona Usener, Alma Wahrmund, and Alma Wunderlich. The men are: Hugo Ahrens, August Arlt, Hans Basse, Hugo Henke, Max Henke, Louis Henke, Rudolf Kott, Wilhelm Kuhlmann, Otto Mueller, Felix Otte, Berthold Pfiester, Max Ransleben, Wilhelm Seelig, Max Weirich, and Otto Wunderlich. The Pastor is thought to be Pastor G. Howe.

Opposite Page: These two youngsters dressed in their Sunday finest, Sidney Matthew Metzger and Oscar William Metzger, are seen seated at the Marienkirche circa 1904. Little Sidney later became Bishop Metzger of El Paso. Courtesy of Oscar F. Metzger.

These ladies started quilting in 1921 at the Holy Ghost Lutheran Church. This 1951 photo is of their thirtieth anniversary. The Holy Ghost quilting group, which is still quilting today, made quilts on request from individuals and organizations in the community. Payment for the quilts would be made to the church as a donation. Seated from left to right are: Mrs. Max Moellering, Mrs. Otto Kolmeier, Mrs. August Weber, Mrs. Eugene Schmidt, Mrs. Walter Henke, and Mrs. Berthold Pfiester. Standing from left to right are: Mrs. Louis Kordzik, Mrs. William Schneider, Mrs. Cornelia Alberthal, Mrs. O. Lindenberg, Mrs. Alfred Schmidt, Mrs. Rud. Schnappauf, Mrs. Wesley Franz, Mrs. Katie Seelig, Mrs. Arthur Crenwelge Sr., Mrs. Emil Wahrmund, Mrs. Emilie Doebbler, Mrs. Arnold Klinksiek, and Mrs. Edgar Stroeher. Courtesy of Holy Ghost Lutheran Church.

In 1955 the former Bethany Lutheran Church was dedicated as First Baptist Church. The Building Committee, from left to right are: Earl Coplen, Mrs. Otto Hohmann, Otto Hohmann, Rev. J. M. Garner, Varnell Bartholmae, and J. Luther Watson. In the second row are: R. H. Morris, C. R. Crittenden, Max Schneider. B. H. Heinen, and Marvin Daniel. Courtesy of First Baptist Church.

The first Catholic services were held in 1847 in the home of Johann Leyendecker without the assistance of a priest. Later that year a French priest and a Spanish priest arrived and conducted services in one of the Society's buildings. There the first Mass was read and the first sacraments were distributed. In 1848 the congregation bought a plot of land for eighteen dollars and two plots on which there was a house for two hundred dollars. Here a wooden church was fashioned. The first stone for the second building, the Marienkirche, was laid under the leadership of Peter Schandua in 1861. Peter Schandua is seen here at a church celebration at the building he helped build. Courtesy of Geraldine Dittmar.

The old Marienkirche encased in the lovely wrought iron fence provided a good resting place for these two young people. Note the dirt streets circa 1920. Courtesy of the Stonewall Heritage Foundation.

Harper's first Catholic Church founded in 1909. Courtesy of the Stonewall Heritage Foundation.

The young people of First Baptist Church help prepare for the building dedication service February 17, 1955. Courtesy of First Baptist Church.

Frederick William Schnerr, a nobleman from Germany, fell in love with a common maid. Because marriage was impossible for them, they left Germany and made their home in Gillespie County. Schnerr, like most aristocrats, was unfamiliar with work and it is said that all duties fell to his wife, Emma Elizabeth. When she died in 1903, he sought an appropriate tombstone for her grave, disposing of one that did not suit him. He contracted Elisabet Ney to sculpt an angel tombstone. It was the only tombstone she ever sculpted. Ney's work includes statues of Stephen F. Austin and Sam Houston. The tombstone, known as the Elisabet Ney angel, was one of the last works by Ney. Photo © Jeannette Joy Hormouth.

The Harper Presbyterian Church was built in 1900. This picture was taken in 1963 during Harper's Centennial celebration. All four century plants bloomed that season. Courtesy of Harper Historical Society.

In 1978 the building which housed the first Methodist church in the county was purchased by the Gillespie County Historical Society. The building now serves as the central location for all historical society works.

This sketch, titled "Dutch House" in Fredericksburg, Texas, was done by Seth Eastman on January 29, 1849. The sketch illustrates the transition from a log cabin to a fachwerk house. The house in the foreground was probably built first and then the fachwerk, or half timber house built later. Courtesy of the McNay Museum of Art, San Antonio, through a gift of the Pearl Brewing Company.

Chapter Three

The County's Architecture

"Not so long after moving to this place my father died, leaving my mother with nine children . . . on her hands. We lived in a one room log house. That wasn't so bad in the wintertime and during the dark of the moon, but in hot weather and moonshine nights it was the limit of discomfort. In dark nights enduring the hot weather we might leave a door open and sleep with one eye shut, but during the moonshine nights we had to keep the door closed and bolted from the inside. The Indians always did their marauding during the moonlight . . ."

—BIGGERS

When the settlers first arrived, their most pressing need aside from food was shelter. Before returning to New Braunfels, the Adelsverein troopers who had assisted the pioneers on their journey from New Braunfels helped the settlers fashion tents and brush arbors to serve as a temporary shelter from the elements. The settlers then quickly constructed Mexican Jacals, huts covered with grass. Although the structures were primitive, the tall grass kept out the rain. The settlers lived in these rough shelters until they were able to build log cabins or other, more substantial homes.

While still in Germany, the settlers had received information from travel guides promoting the log cabin as the home of choice in the new land. Some of the travel guides circulating in Germany even came complete with building tips. The log cabin, which played a brief but enduring part of the settlement of Gillespie County, was a novelty to the German settlers and not typical of German architecture.

Building tips may have been encouraging in Germany, but once in Texas, the settlers soon discovered it was not tips they needed, but a strong back. Walnut and oak for the settlers' log cabins were abundant, but they still faced the daunting tasks of chopping and hand hewing the logs for their new shelters. The size of the logs dictated the size of the cabin.

Of course these newcomers were anything but seasoned frontiersmen and occasionally something seemingly simple, like chopping down a tree, could cause a great amount of consternation. "One day Reverend Basse went into the woods to get a tree trunk. He found a tree that suited him and, so that the falling tree might load itself onto the wagon, he moved the wagon into proper position close to the tree. He also fastened a rope to the tree top to enable him to lower the tree gently and began to chop. Soon the tree began to reel and lean toward the wagon. Mr. Basse seized the rope but was unable to hold it and the tree crashed down on the wagon. Mr. Basse, a wiser man, had to take his team home and salvage his wagon piece by piece" (Penniger) Obviously, being a pioneer did not necessarily come naturally.

After the settlers cleared and cultivated their land and had

Opposite page: Albert Keidel's early efforts in the 1930s and beyond to restore old rock structures and turn them into modern homes inspired many others to do the same. He has been acknowledged as a forerunner to the renovation work that is being done throughout the state of Texas. The wardrobe in the background is an original handcrafted piece by Johann Peter Tatsch of Fredericksburg. Photo taken by John Lewis Stage for *Town & Country* magazine, courtesy of Mrs. J. Hardin Perry.

Johann Peter Tatsch, expert cabinetmaker, built this home in 1856 out of local stone. Visitors have long been fascinated by the huge double fireplace. Detailed floor plans of the house were placed in the Library of Congress.

The J. J. Knopp home was first built in 1871. In the 1930s it was restored by Albert Keidel. This was one of the first examples of restoration work on the older rock structures. Today these homes are in high demand and have strong retail value. Courtesy of Mrs. J. Hardin Perry.

an adequate food supply, efforts turned toward building more refined and permanent homes. The log cabin had served its function, but now the Germans returned to their native styles and methods of building. The humble cabin took its place on the homestead as the barn or became a part of a bigger structure.

A typical mode of construction in Germany was fachwerk, or half timber. The settlers framed their fachwerk houses with post oak. The spaces between the framing timbers were filled with stone or occasionally, as was the case at Fort Martin Scott, adobe bricks. Then, if the owner's economic means allowed, he plastered the outside of the building, often leaving the timbers exposed. Hand-split cypress shingles were used for roofing. Occasionally the side of the building was also covered with shingles to protect the structure from weathering. Many of the windows, floorboards, and doors for the new edifices were purchased from the Mormon mill which existed for a short time on the Pedernales River.

During the same period some of the Germans also built with rock. Many of these rock structures were constructed of limestone that was quarried from the Cross Mountain vicinity.

Because limestone is soft in its natural form, and later hardens, it made an ideal building material. Generally, the settlers made lime on site to join the limestone permanently. Gun portals were frequently placed within the rock walls of outbuildings and fences, enabling the first settlers to defend themselves against the Indians.

These early homes were typically a story and a half with one room, a lean-to and an attached porch. The lean-to served as a kitchen. But occasionally the kitchen would be placed in an entirely different building in order to prevent an overzealous cook from burning down the house. Many of the houses had an exterior stairway with the upstairs being used for sleeping quarters for the children or for storage.

The German home was neat and tidy with shutters on the windows. The yards were enclosed with picket fences. Rather than having grass grow in the yard, they kept it raked, swept, and free from any overgrowth. This barren lawn approach was an efficient means for protecting homes from grass fires.

Only one of the Fredericksburg residents, Joseph Martin, was listed in the 1850 census as an architect, but many of the other residents were stonemasons, carpenters, and cabinetmakers. These trades required not only great skill, but also a certain amount of artistry. The work of these craftsmen is evident in the architecture and cabinetry that remains in the community today.

Cabinetmaker Johann Peter Tatsch was one of those skilled craftsmen. Because of the quality and precision of his work, his pieces were in high demand. He built everything from custom sized spinning wheels to large wardrobes. By the end of his life, handcrafted furniture fell out of favor and mass produced furniture grew in demand. His own daughter was

Located on the corner of San Antonio and Crockett Streets in Fredericksburg, was the Pfeil blacksmith shop and home. The building was designed to enable a wagon to go through the front door and out the through the back door. After years of service the old home was restored and now serves as a beautiful residence. Photo taken circa 1800s, courtesy of Vickie Swanson.

Built in the 1900s the Kuenemann House on Creek and Edison Streets in Fredericksburg is a good example of the bigger homes that were built after the Civil War when milled wood lumber was more accessible. Courtesy of Paul Hamilton.

said to have desired a factory-made bedroom suite for her new home when she married. Today, however, fine craftsmanship triumphs. Many Tatsch pieces are still in excellent condition and being used and cherished as a piece of Gillespie County's history.

After the Civil War order and peace finally came to the county. Mass milled lumber became much more accessible, and consequently, the architectural style changed. Now builders had local access to windows, gingerbread trim, picket fences, and flooring. With that access came a flurry of houses built in the Victorian Style, and Victorian details were added to existing structures. Interestingly, the homes were not overly ornate, perhaps due to German practicality.

As the community grew and fears of the Indians dissipated, many of the settlers moved to the outskirts of town where they had more property. Some of these settlers also built small, simple homes close to the church or maintained their original homesteads. Then when they came into town for church, they had a place to stay. Often more than one family shared the house. Those small second homes came to be called "Sunday Houses." Several of the Sunday Houses are still in existence today and often give rest to weary travelers, now as guest houses or bed and breakfasts. The quaint Sunday House, featured in a variety of publications, has proved to be fascinating for visitors and has become a must see landmark.

During the first half of the twentieth century, the architecture in the county became thoroughly "Americanized." No longer were the structures influenced by the settlers' German heritage as much as by the building trends across the country. By the middle of the twentieth century, many people had lost interest in the county's original buildings. Landowners and businessmen often found it easier to raze an older building and replace it with a modern facility rather than attempting to rejuvenate the old edifices. Destruction was the fate of many landmarks. Even the county's second courthouse, which was designed and built at great expense to the county, was once doomed to be razed. However, some residents of Gillespie County had a deep appreciation for structures with historical value and fought to preserve them. Often when complete restoration wasn't feasible, doors, hardware and logs were salvaged for later use. Fortunately, due to the efforts and finances of various friends of the county, many buildings survived destruction, including the old courthouse which now houses Pioneer Memorial Library. A debt of gratitude is owed to those who fought to preserve a part of the county's heritage.

Today the historical buildings are in high demand. And builders in the community are attempting to replicate and remodel the county's original German architecture. Indeed, this is a tribute to the early craftsman and builders of Gillespie County.

View of Fredericksburg's Main Street architecture in the year 1910. The old bank building was one of four buildings designed by Alfred Giles in Gillespie County. Courtesy of the *Standard*.

The Willie Knopp, Jr., family at their home built circa 1900. Willie Knopp and Emma Weidenfeller Knopp (pictured) were the parents of eight children who all slept upstairs. The home remains in the family and serves as a place of refuge and reminiscing. Courtesy of Janette Kroger.

The lot the Priess building was built upon changed hands many times, once being sold for a mere eleven dollars. The German Immigration Society owned it as well as a tailor and a wheelwright. In 1878 Charles Priess purchased the lot and built a combination home and business. He and his family lived upstairs. The building was constructed out of limestone quarried near the Bear Mountain Road. The store was a general merchandise and hardware store. Priess was also an agent for Lone Star Beer Company and part of the basement was used to store beer. Many years later in 1919 Dr. Victor Keidel purchased the building and had it converted to a hospital. The Priess building was renovated by Albert Keidel with the assistance of architect Edward Stein in 1938. The building served as a hospital until 1973. Today it is used by Dr. Victor Keidel's son-in-law, Dr. J. Hardin Perry, and his associates as a family practice clinic. The Keidel family has served the community with four generations of physicians. Courtesy of Mrs. J. Hardin Perry.

The William Bierschwale home was completed in 1889. This stately home remained in the family for nearly one hundred years. William Bierschwale and his wife, Lina Jung Bierschwale, contracted Alfred Giles, an English architect from San Antonio, who also designed Pioneer Memorial Library. With fine attention to detail, Giles designed a grand home with walls over twenty inches thick. The bedrooms were located upstairs enabling them to enjoy the breeze. Visible in the background is the old windmill. Pictured from top left is the Bierschwale family: Henry, Ernest, Max, Walter B., Alfred, Cordie, William, Annie, Oma Jung, Mrs. William Bierschwale, Eugene, and Edna Jung. Photo taken in 1899, courtesy of Peggy Johnson.

The Thiele's enjoyed the benefit of having generous friends and neighbors in a fifties style house raisin'. The Thiele family received help from friends, family, and neighbors as they constructed their house in 1952 on Thiele Lane. Pictured from the left are: Hulda Thiele, Mildred Wilke (holding Iris Fiedler Burrer), Lauren Fiedler (holding Elaine Wilke Baiglsley) Cary Wilke, Christine Behrends, Francis Fiedler, and Eugene Behrends (background, William Thiele by car). To this day only members of the Thiele family live on this road. Courtesy of Norman and Mildred Wilke.

The oldest home in Fredericksburg was built by Johann Jost Klingelhoefer in 1847. He and his family received this town lot and immediately took possession of the land. They set up a tent and there the family lived while he began efforts toward building a sturdy home. And sturdy it was. It was built in the typical fashion employing the fachwerk technique. The lean-to on the back end of the house was added after the Civil War. His son, Julius Klingelhoefer, married Sophia Tatsch, daughter of Peter Tatsch, the expert cabinetmaker. This enabled the couple to furnish the home with Tatsch's works of art. Courtesy of Reuben and Margaret Kammlah.

Alfred Giles, a highly reputable architect from San Antonio, was hired when the need arose for a new courthouse. The goal was to build a beautiful building out of native material. That goal was met in 1882. The stone came from about 2 1/2 miles northeast of town, the best lumber was used, along with intricate locks and doorknobs. The building was heated by wood stoves. Note the windmill and water tank. In 1896 electricity was added. In 1966-67 the building was renovated primarily through the donations of Mr. and Mrs. Eugene McDermott. The building was then dedicated as a library in 1967 with First Lady Lady Bird Johnson present. Courtesy of George Vogel.

This old board and batten Sunday house was built in 1890. The photo, taken from the back, shows the steeple of St. Mary's to the right. Like most Sunday houses it was built close to the church. The tank on the left was used for gathering rainwater for bathing. Pictured from the left are: Leroy, Elmer, Ernst, Ida, and Jane Wahrmund. The family used the house when they came into town. The other two people, Alvin and Emma Juenke, were renters. The building was later torn down and used for a barn and today the lot stands vacant. Photo taken in 1937, courtesy of Elmer Wahrmund.

This photo shows the typical story-and-a-half house with a lean-to in the back and shutters on the windows. Generally the lean-to was used as a kitchen and the porch added later. The porch was not typical to German architecture and shows the influence of the early American houses on the German builders. Seen in the photo from the left are Adolf Max and Sophie Marschall Usener. Adolf taught school in the Live Oak Community. Photo taken in 1896, courtesy of Marcella Britton.

The White Elephant Saloon on Main Street in Fredericksburg was built in 1888 by John Kleck. He and his family lived in a frame house behind the saloon for many years. At the rear of the rock building was a two-story frame addition that was used as the upper room for high-stakes gambling. The games played for smaller stakes took place downstairs. During its history the saloon changed ownership several times and went through many physical changes. When the Sunday laws were enacted, the business simply locked its front doors and left the back doors open for customers. The white elephant and the wrought ironwork that crowns the old building lend a regal air that tourists and locals alike enjoy. Today a weaving shop is located in this building. Courtesy of Mrs. J. Hardin Perry.

This house was one of two identical houses built for two brothers who married two sisters, Felix and Hattie Keidel and Kurt and Margaret Keidel. Photo taken circa 1915, courtesy of RoShell Baker.

The Loeffler-Weber home had its humble beginnings as a log home built in 1846-47. In 1867 a cooking fireplace and rock and fachwerk rooms were added. The house remained in the family for ninety years. Loeffler, a cabinetmaker, used the lean-to as his workshop. He made furniture and, like other cabinetmakers of the day, coffins. When the house was restored in the 1960s by Gloria and George Hill, a child's coffin was found in the loft. The new owners donated the coffin to the Gillespie County Historical Society where it can be seen as a part of the colorful past in the Pioneer Museum today.
Courtesy of Mrs. J. Hardin Perry.

This stately ranch house was built after the Civil War. Charlie and Wanda Evers lived in it for fifty-five years.
Photo taken 1895, courtesy of Bessie Evers.

This was a lucky day for Charlie Evers. He killed this eight point whitetail trophy deer on their ranch around 1902. Courtesy of Bessie Evers.

This photo shows a view of Fredericksburg's Main Street during the county's first fifty years. The building to the far right was, at that time, a bar. The building was later covered with a stone facade and is presently Security State Bank. To the left is the first courthouse. Further left is the "modern courthouse" which is now the Pioneer Memorial Library. Shown in the center is the Vereins Kirche surrounded by arbors put up to protect citizens and animals from the blistering heat. Note also the hitching posts. Courtesy of Geraldine Walch Dittmar.

This is the Mund home at the turn of the century. It is located in the Doss/Cherry Spring area and is typical of the homesteads in the county. Note the log cabin to the left of the farm house. The plaster is crumbling in some parts, exposing the original logs. Typically, the log cabin was the first home built, followed by a better made, wooden framed home. Courtesy of the Mund family.

This house is a good example of the Victorian style that was prominent at the turn of the century. It is located at the corner of North Orange and West Travis Streets in Fredericksburg. Courtesy of the *Standard*.

Creek Street—the way it was. The house on the far left is known as the Kuenemann house. Next to it stands a lumber mill. Aside from Stein Lumber Company, this lumber mill was the only other in Fredericksburg. The house was recently restored to its former grandeur, now with the welcome addition of tall trees. Courtesy of Paul Hamilton.

This cabin is now located in the Harper Community park but was originally constructed in the Spring Creek area in the 1860s. Near the cabin, in the back right, is a well that was hand dug by Jim Morris, Tom Harlan, Sr., and Mr. Dixon in 1882. Courtesy of Harper Historical Society.

After original buildings in the county ran their course of usefulness, many were razed. The case of the Vereins Kirche was no different. In 1897, after the community celebrated its fiftieth anniversary, down came the original octagonal building. However, unlike other razed structures, the county decided to build another, a replica of the original Vereins Kirche. Today's Vereins Kirche stands in the center of Marktplatz off Main Street in Fredericksburg. The original structure stood directly in the middle of Main Street. Courtesy of the *Standard*.

The E. Maier building was one of the first two-story buildings on Main Street in Fredericksburg. The building is located on the corner of Main and South Adams, directly across the street from the courthouse circa 1890. Courtesy of the *Standard*.

Security State Bank, on the corner of Crockett and Main Street in Fredericksburg, was once the Plaza Hotel. To the left of the Plaza is the construction of the new U.S. Post Office and is the location of the original courthouse. Through the construction, you can see the second courthouse for Gillespie County which is now the Pioneer Memorial Library. Courtesy of the *Standard*.

This is Lyne Klingelhoefer Lewis Harper's sketch of the Kammlah House, now the Gillespie County Historical Society's Pioneer Museum. The Society bought the house and surrounding property in 1955 and has since developed a large collection of historical artifacts from the county. Sketch used with permission of Lyne Klingelhoefer Lewis Harper.

Victorian details were often added to older structures after the Civil War. This house was originally built shortly after the property was purchased by Albert Lee Patton in 1876. Courtesy of John Haebig.

Although Gillespie County's second courthouse was nearly doomed to be destroyed, with the help of donors the building was restored. These men work hard to get the job done. Courtesy of the *Standard*.

Goats of every variety have been a vital aspect of the livestock industry in Gillespie County. In 1936 Adolf Stieler poses with his goats in a General Motors promotion promoting the mohair seats of the car. Stieler raised large numbers of goats and was hailed by *Life Magazine* as the "Goat King of the World." Stieler donated the first starting gate for the Gillespie County Fair Race Track. Courtesy Shatzie Crouch.

Chapter Four

Improving the Land

Once the brave Germans had decided to emigrate, thoughts turned more and more toward their future in the new land. The emigrants were an eclectic group of farmers, doctors, lawyers, ministers, craftsmen, and artists, and the new settlement needed all their various skills. Nevertheless, necessity dictated that all settlers become tillers of the soil merely to survive. Knowing the need to farm, the Adelsverein told the settlers to pack seeds, but leave their farming implements behind—they would be purchased in America. How brave those emigrants were to head for unseen destinations with only a satchel of seeds as their tool for future provision.

Upon arriving in Fredericksburg, the first settlers tried their hand at farming by planting a field of corn and a community garden. Even those skilled at farming had to adjust to a new climate, new soils, and the unavailability of appropriate tools. Initially the yield of their crops was limited, resulting in a paltry diet of meat and bread. Consequently a scurvy-type disease claimed many lives. By the time soldiers arrived to construct Fort Martin Scott in 1848, many of the settlers were on the verge of starvation. Nonetheless, the determined settlers forged onward.

It wasn't until 1849, as the cholera epidemic raged, that the settlers harvested the first wheat crop and ground it into flour at the Mormon's gristmill. The Mormons had settled on the Pedernales and seemed better versed at farming. Their temporary assistance to the settlement proved invaluable.

Cotton was the major cash crop in Gillespie County from the 1870s until the boll weevil could not be controlled in the 1920s. This picture, taken in the early 1920s, shows cotton being picked by hand on the Hugo and Anna Gold Crenwelge farm in the Rheingold community. Courtesy of Ken Crenwelge.

Ironically, the Mormon settlement dwindled and later disappeared after its mill was destroyed in a flood.

Hardship had come close to destroying the fledgling community, and yet when the dark cloud lifted, the surviving settlers embraced the work at hand and sought ways to improve the village. It was recorded in Penniger's fiftieth anniversary book that a Mr. Spechte became involved with the U.S. Department of Agriculture. He introduced rye and wheat seeds to the local farmers which led to the opening of several mills.

In the 1870s seeds of the kingly crop called cotton fell into the weathered hands of Gillespie County farmers. This cash crop grew so large that at one time seventeen cotton gins operated in Gillespie County, and the New York Stock Exchange maintained a cotton futures board office in Fredericksburg. But soaring with the royal crop lasted only a few years. In the 1920s, the boll weevil brought calamity to the cotton farmer. Meetings were called, and solutions sought, but to no avail. The small pestilence defeated cotton in Gillespie County.

While the cotton industry floundered, Gillespie County received its first county extension agent, Henry F. Grote. He encouraged the farmers to diversify their crops. This advice was not only good for business, but also good for the soil. His foresight, coupled with the farmers' tenacity, helped bring the county through the cotton industry's collapse.

Of course the weather was then as it is today, the farmers' friend and foe. During the Depression, for example, one of the worst droughts plagued the county's farmers and ranchers. Many ranchers participated in a federal program which allowed government agents to come onto individual ranches and slaughter cattle. According to one local rancher, who was a young man at the time, cattle were slaughtered for $1.50 per head. The rancher could then double his earnings by selling the hide of the animal at a government counting facility. Many of today's county residents still remember the dry and dismal days of the cattle slaughters.

After living through the drought, dust bowl days, and the Depression, the hearty bunch of Gillespie County farmers and ranchers were ready for a new agriculture venture—peanuts. The county was allotted hundreds of acres by the government for peanut production during the Roosevelt administration. The program required each farmer to produce a certain amount of peanuts in order to receive land allocation payments the following year. Though productive, the peanut industry was short lived in Gillespie County. There was a great deal of labor involved and the peanuts had to be harvested at exactly the right time, which often occurred during the rainiest part of the year. In the meantime, peanut prices plummeted and several of the farmers experienced root rot—a consequence of over planting. The industry waned considerably by World War II, and by the 1950s, the peanut chapter of Gillespie County agriculture was closed. Aside from the unfavorable soil and climate conditions for peanut production, the pay was, as some would say, peanuts.

Baling peanut hay in Rocky Hill Community in 1942 was hard work. Pictured from the left are: Willie Behrends, Clara Hartmann, Francis Hartmann, Edward Hartmann, and Patricia Gellermann holding a granddaughter. The baler is a 1942 Case power baler, and the car is a 1926 Dodge. Courtesy of Jeanette Klein.

Meanwhile, ranchers were perpetually besieged by the screw worm. The screw worm was the hatched larvae of the blow fly, which laid its eggs in open wounds on cattle and other livestock. Once hatched, the worms ate the flesh of the animals. Ranchers were faced with the constant labor of keeping watch over their livestock and nursing the animals infected with the loathsome larvae. Until the late 1950s, this problem went on unabated. Because the female blowfly had the ability to mate only once, a government program was developed to create sterile male blowflies. Airplanes dropped the sterile blowflies above each rancher's herd, enabling the female blowfly to mate with the sterile male, thus ending the screwworm cycle. Over time, the pestilence was completely eradicated, much to the ranchers' relief.

Although the farmers and ranchers were not free from hard times, successful agricultural endeavors sprouted and grew to make lasting marks on the Gillespie County agriculture scene. The peach industry, for example, was started in the 1920s by a high school teacher, B. L. Enderle. Others saw the success he was experiencing and ventured into the fruit growing realm. Today an abundance of peach growers in the county is

This hunting campsite is located on the Lewis Ranch, also known as the Conrad Welge homestead which is in the northwest part of Gillespie County between Doss and Cherry Springs. Pictured from the left are: William C. Lewis, Mr. Merriwether, the camp supervisor, and Jack C. Lewis. In the background sits the hunters' "cook" tent. Courtesy of William C. Lewis.

Peanut harvest in Rocky Hill Community in 1931. Standing by the truck are Carl Roos on the left and Edward Hartmann on the right. Courtesy of Jeanette Klein.

evidenced by the many roadside stands that dot Highways 290, 87, and 16. Peach crops not only survived the rough years, they thrived over the long haul, making Gillespie County the leading peach producing county in the state of Texas. Today, in the summertime, many a traveler heads for Gillespie County strictly to buy peaches.

Months later, in the fall, another important and successful venture in Gillespie County occurs with the arrival of hundreds of hunters. Many ranchers supplement their agricultural endeavors by leasing land to hunting sportsmen from Texas and beyond, drawn to the area after turkeys and other small game, but especially the white-tailed deer. The influx of hunters has greatly benefited the local economy.

In the past one hundred and fifty years, versatility has been the trademark for the farmer and rancher in Gillespie County. He has had to be steadfast, flexible, and patient. The weather has been unpredictable, livestock prices have gone up and down, and yet many residents in Gillespie County still own land ranched by their forefathers. They press on like their ancestors, taking pride in being stewards of the land.

Taming the touchy prickly pear seemed to be an ongoing effort. John Lewis used fuel in 1937 to get the job done. This pear burning endeavor was usually done during the dry season when there was little or no grass for the cattle to eat. After the thorns were burned, the cattle were able to eat the cactus. Once the rains came, and the grass was again plentiful, it became difficult to keep the cattle from eating the cactus. This is still done today generally with a four wheeler and a propane tank. Courtesy of William C. Lewis.

Felix E. Pfiester and Alfred Pfiester threshing in the field in 1916. Courtesy of Adele Duecker.

Threshing oats on the Wanda and Charlie Evers Ranch at Salt Branch in the 1920s. One time, after heavy rains, the tractor was water logged in the field for three weeks before it could be removed. Courtesy of Bessie E. Evers.

The Pfeil Gin in the early 1900s was built by G. A. Pfeil on "Orphan's Land." The gin, which was bought by his sons Otto and Felix, became the Pfeil Brothers Gin. The brothers maintained the symbol of the arrow, the English equivalent to the German word, "Pfeil." Courtesy of Vicki Swanson.

Alfred Sauer uses the harrow on his farm at Doss in 1917. This piece of farming equipment was drawn by a mule or horse and used to level plowed ground. Courtesy of Dora Stein.

Sixteen-year-old Charlie Evers endures his lonely vigil at the Schaefer House (shepherd's house) at Salt Branch. Young Charlie spent weeks at a time at the camphouse tending the sheep for his father, Ludwig Evers. Courtesy of Bessie E. Evers.

Pictured here around 1900 is a horse-drawn pump jack owned by the Lorenz Wendel family, located seven miles northwest of Harper, Texas. Courtesy of Milton Wendel.

Private butchering was a necessity for many years. To make the job a little easier and a perhaps a little more festive, families formed Butcher Clubs. The butchering in Doss took place at Lange's Mill because it was above a creek and therefore the coolest place in the area. Sixteen families participated. Each week one family butchered a cow and divided the meat into sixteen portions, each generally weighing around twenty pounds. The other families then met at Lange's Mill and picked up their portions of the meat. Every week each family received a different part of the beef. This practice took place only during the summer due to lack of refrigeration. In the winter, meat was made into sausage, and the club was discontinued until the following summer. Once each of the families had access to modern refrigeration the club was completely dissolved. Courtesy of Dora Stein.

In the summer of 1900 Carl Priess, along with his nine-year-old-son Charlie, went to Comfort to pick up their new threshing machine (shown in photo) which had been shipped by train from Racine, Wisconsin. The Priesses were among the first people in the Luckenbach community to own a thresher. They threshed their own grain as well as that of their neighbors. It took at least fifteen men and ten horses to thresh the grain. The horses walked in a circle, turning the gears and making the thresher run. The work began as early in the day as possible, though they occasionally had to wait for the stalks to dry after a heavy dew. The neighbors brought their wagons and lent a hand. The women prepared meals and brought cookies and cakes. The men took a morning break and had sandwiches, cake, cookies, and coffee. Before going back to work, each man took a shot of whiskey.

The men each had different tasks. Some loaded hay from the field onto a wagon with a pitch fork. Some fed the thresher with stalks of wheat or oats. Others formed a line to pass the leftover straw along, and stacked it in a neat pile. Two men emptied the buckets of grain, as they were filled, into sacks, which were held open by nine-year-old Charlie. Then everyone helped carry the one hundred fifty pound sacks of grain to the barn.

Because the work was very hard and the men were always quite hungry, they had a very large dinner at noon. In the afternoon the men took another break and ate sandwiches, cake, and cookies. They drank coffee and whiskey and told jokes. Later, the Priess family, like many others, bought machines run by engines rather than horses. Consequently, fewer men were needed to thresh the grain. Eventually, each farmer owned his own combine and only two men were needed to harvest the grain. Although the work became somewhat easier, the men missed the camaraderie of working together. Pictured are Carl Priess, his son Charlie, as well as family members and neighbors. Courtesy of Mrs. Ruby Preiss Arlitt.

The rocky soil and hilly terrain of the Texas Hills are ideal for goats, which have played a part in Gillespie County agriculture for years. The goat industry has centered around angora or mohair goats, but in more recent years meat goats have increased in numbers. Courtesy of Roscoe Basse.

Lange's Mill in Doss serves today as a testament to the fortitude of many of the first settlers. The original mill was founded in the summer of 1856 on the Threadgill Creek by Thomas Doss, John E. Doss, and William C. Thomas. The founding marked the inception of Doss and the birth of the mill now known as Lange's Mill. The Doss brothers experienced only moderate success with the mill. In 1859 a tremendous flood wiped out their dam and washed away their saw and gristmill. Later that same year, fire completely destroyed their home.

Several men tried their hand at getting the mill up and going when finally it settled in the hands of the Lange family in 1866. The Langes also had their fair share of trials while operating the mill. Nevertheless, the Langes persevered. The mill remains in the Lange family complete with a historical marker. Travelers often go out of their way to see this stoutly built shadow of the past. Courtesy of Dennis Lange.

All sorts of skills were necessary to be a productive citizen in Gillespie County. Dr. Victor Keidel (sitting far right) helps with calf roping between house calls. Also pictured from left to right are: Henry Schmidt, Charlie Kott, Mrs. Felix Real, Mrs. Charlie Kott, and Felix Real. Courtesy of Judy Vordenbaum.

Cattle Drives through Main Street were at one time a common occurrence. Today the cattle speed through town in eighteen wheelers, and replacing the cattle herds are hordes of tourists. Courtesy of the *Standard*.

Enjoying a drink of either homemade wine or beer in front of the tank house are, from left to right: Berthold, Edward, Felix, Benno, Alfred, and Frida Pfiester. The tank house stood next to the windmill and the tank on top stored water. By having the tank above ground the pull of gravity on the water gave the owners running water. Often bathing facilities were placed inside the tank house. Until the city incorporated, each homestead had a hand dug well and then later cisterns and windmills. Courtesy of Adele Duecker.

In 1916 prior to the widespread use of the diesel engine, steam powered the way. The two men in the tractor are thought to be Alfred and Felix Pfiester. Mrs. Felix Pfiester looks on from the Model T with children Adolph, Adele, Alma, and Lydia. Courtesy of Adele Duecker.

Harvest time in the late 1920s was often a family affair. From left to right: August, Anna, Lottie and George Eberle show the fruit of their labors. Courtesy of August Eberle.

Although the "modern" farming equipment was quicker, more efficient, and perhaps easier than threshing, the farmer may have missed the companionship that came with the older machinery. Courtesy of the Stonewall Heritage Society.

Little Boy Blue come blow your horn . . . Emil Henry Sauer contemplates life on the farm in the sheep pens. Courtesy of Dora Stein.

A farmer's social life was often interwoven with his work. Here men and boys rest on cotton bales at the gin and delight in their harvest. Courtesy of the *Standard*.

Since the 1920s peaches have been a major cash crop in Gillespie County. A man walks through an orchard in Stonewall and inspects the crop. Courtesy of Stonewall Heritage Society.

People who raised chickens brought eggs into Farmer's Grain in Fredericksburg. Farmer's Grain purchased the eggs, checked to see if they were fertile, and then packaged them to be sold. Photo taken circa 1948, courtesy of the Stonewall Heritage Society.

Kenneth Kunz inspects the newcomers to his family's turkey farm. Raising turkeys in Gillespie County has been a steady enterprise over the years. Backyard turkey flocks later turned into large turkey farms. The growing interest in raising turkeys led to the opening of the turkey plant in 1958. Today there are approximately fifteen turkey farms in the county and the turkey plant processes around three million turkeys a year with three hundred employees. Courtesy of Stonewall Heritage Society.

Participation in the 4-H program is a long-time tradition for children in Gillespie County. This young lady gives an earnest effort as she shows her pig in 1992. Courtesy of the *Standard*.

Left: Cattle were dipped regularly during the thirties and forties in order to keep the Texas fever tick in check. The vat was filled with a medicated liquid and the cattle were brought by cattle drives from area ranches to private or community vats in order to receive the treatment. Courtesy of Mrs. J. Hardin Perry.

Henry Beckmann, John Pehl, Charlie Weinheimer, and James Eckert enjoy themselves at the Stonewall Community Fair in 1956. Courtesy of the Stonewall Heritage Society.

Wool Show Harper, Texas - 1948

Posing for a photo during threshing was a liberty rarely taken. Courtesy of Stonewall Heritage Society.

Opposite bottom: Men and women gathered in Harper, Texas, to watch the Wool Show in 1948. Wool and mohair production was a significant revenue generator for ranchers for many years. Courtesy of KNAF.

This photo of four seasoned couples was taken September 9, 1935, at Mr. and Mrs. Pete Metzger's fiftieth anniversary celebration. All of the couples were married fifty years or more. Seated from left to right are: Mr. and Mrs. John Metzger (married fifty-seven years), Mr. and Mrs. Adam Metzger (married fifty-four years), Mr. and Mrs. Peter Metzger (married fifty years), and Mr. and Mrs. Joe Hartmann (married fifty-one years). Courtesy of Fritz Metzger.

Chapter Five

Social Life in the County

"Leave Germany and come here where you can live happily and contentedly. If you work only half as much as in Germany, you can live without troubles in every sense of the word we are free . . . We still live so remote from other people that we are lonely, but we have dances, churches and schools . . . Do not let anyone persuade you to go to any other place than Fredericksburg."
    —Letter from Fredericksburg, 1850
    Peter Birk in *The German Texans*, Glen E. Lich, page 57

In the first few years of the settlement, the settlers forged deep friendships as they leaned upon one another in times of need and sorrow. Many of the settlers gathered together at church meetings held at the Vereins Kirche for weekly encouragement and companionship.

In due course the cloud lifted from the newly formed county. The Germans were a sociable group, as well as hardworking, and once the settlement was on its feet the people began forming a variety of social organizations. The first *Klubs*, or clubs, included the Turn Verein, an exclusive gymnastic club, choirs, shooting clubs, and quilting groups. Many in the community were interested in intellectual development. For those with that bent the ever popular Casino Club was formed as well as literary clubs and one club specifically for the exchange and expression of ideas.

Before the advent of motorized farming implements and electricity, the people of the county enjoyed one another's company as they worked together in the field, hunted, or quilted. When time allowed, more light hearted entertainment was sought such as dancing, playing cards, or simply sharing coffee. As the years rolled on a silent movie theater became a welcome form of recreation.

Visitors to the county were enamored with the unique community which had retained so much of its heritage. The fact that the German language was so prevalent added to the intrigue. German continued to be spoken, with almost all of the homes being bi-lingual, until the onset of World War II. The community remained tightly knit and it wasn't until the late 1960s that large numbers of people began moving to the county. The new arrivals were met with some hesitancy by longtime Fredericksburg residents, but in time, they became an integral part of the community. The county has continued to grow in numbers, and yet Gillespie County still retains much of its original flavor, and its love of social life.

The Henry Braeutigam family picnic in 1908. Courtesy of Carolyn Montgomery.

Dances were one of the primary social functions in Gillespie County for many years. Each week the various dances were listed in the paper with the time and the band that was playing. The Rhythm Kings played at dances throughout the county. Pictured from left to right are: Woodrow Gold, Marvin Gold, Alfred Duecker, Jimmy Schneider, Harvey Gold, Wesley Heiman, and Oliver Kowert, circa 1930. Courtesy of Adele Duecker.

This is thought to be the White Elephant Saloon circa 1900. It is a typical scene of the local saloons at that time. Not only did the men enjoy a drink in the saloon they also gathered socially to play billiards, cards, and dominoes. Courtesy of Darlene Stehle.

Opposite: German Theatre and Concert Program "Little Theatre Group" Concert on May 7, 1922. Courtesy of Corrine Stehling Danysh.

Großes deutsches Theater und Konzert
— in —
Peters Opernhaus
— am —

1922

Sonntag Abend, den 7ten Mai, Anfang 8:15

Programm

1. March "Down the Line" .... Chas. Wenn
   Blum's Orchester
2. Lied: „Humoristisches Ragaut" .... Männerchor
3. Schwank in einem Akt: „Der Wirrwarr."
   Personen:

Gottfried Hagen, Bürgermeister .... Robert Blum
Gertrud, seine Frau .... Frl. Minna Zenner
Emma, beider Tochter .... Frl. Emmie Blum
Balduin Brausepulver, Apotheker .... Felix Stehling
Schmitt, Leutnant .... John W. Metzger
Johann, sein Bursche .... Alvin Stehling
Kati, Dienstmädchen .... Frl. Helene Stehling

4. Overture "The Old Folks Carnival" .... L. L. Coffin
   Blum's Orchester
5. Lied: „Nachtigall und Rose" .... Gemischter Chor
6. Musikalischer Vortrag: "Face to Face"—Violin: Frls. Dora Knopp, Ida und Margaret Blum; Cornet: Frl. Emmie Blum; Piano Begleitung: Frl. Lottie Stehling
7. Waltz "Love's Awakening" .... A Karger
   Blum's Orchester
8. Schwank in einem Akt: „Der neue Verein"
   Personen:

Zacharias Klumpke, Rentier .... Joe Molberg
Laura, seine Frau .... Frau G. M. Hartmann
Martha Winterfuß, Dienstmädchen .... Frl. Cora Meckel
Frau Hitzkopf .... Frau J. G. Wehmeyer
Frau Kühnemund .... Frau Emil Schandua
Frau Haberbier .... Frau Felix Stehling
Egon Klipperich, Professor .... Henry Kunz

Eintritt: 20 Cents für Kinder, 30 Cents für Erwachsene; Reservierte Sitze 40 Cents.

Reservierte Sitze sind jetzt zu haben in Blum's Store und Peter's Confectionery.

Dr. Victor Keidel takes a break on his ranch and hunts turkeys. Dr. Keidel listened to KNAF radio station at noon when he was at the ranch to keep abreast of any emergencies in town that might require his attention. Courtesy of Judy Vordenbaum.

The Baethges and friends gathered at the dam built below their home on the Live Oak Creek circa 1914. The county built the dam using lime for mortar to prevent erosion when there were torrential rains. Seated from left to right on the bottom row are: Alfred Rusche, Minna Baethge Rusche, Ferdinand Baethege, Louise (Eckert) Baethge, Hugo Baethge, and Lena Baethge. Courtesy of Mrs. Florine Wendel.

The first man from the left behind the bar is Otto Meurer, the owner of this saloon, the Buckhorn at 201 West Main Street. Courtesy of Mrs. Paul Kraus.

Arthur Jenschke, Ferdinand Meier, Alvin Maenius Jr., Hugo Maenius (owner), George Maenius, and Alvin Maenius Sr. share good times and a brew in 1952 at the Albert Saloon, in Albert, Texas. Courtesy of Norman and Mildred Wilke.

The Railroad Bridge on the Old San Antonio Highway proved to be a popular meeting place for young people during the twenties. The young man standing in the center is Felix William Baethge. Courtesy of Florine Wendel.

The Luckenbach family enjoys old fashioned fun at the fishing hole on John Wendel's property at Cherry Springs. The water hole was called the *wasserfalle* or waterfall by the family. Courtesy of Roscoe and Dorothy Basse.

Engel's Store was a place for socializing in Luckenbach in the late 1800s. Enjoying themselves in the late 1890s are Albert Pehl, George Weber, Mr. Havorkannm, Willie Baag, Willie Engel, Walter Engel, Willie Burg, and Theodore Pehl. Courtesy of Jeanette Klein.

The family reunion continues to be a tradition in Gillespie County. Oftentimes a general announcement of the upcoming reunion is made via the newspaper or radio. In 1936 the Ferdinand Baethge family gathered at Klaerner's Park. Courtesy of Florine Wendel.

Occasionally KNAF would broadcast live bands. The Starlighter Band was organized in 1946 and played for all occasions. The band was comprised of Lorenz Schuch, Albert Brodbeck, Harry Ahrens, Norman Thiele, Heinrich Friedrich, and Lillian Grona. This photo was taken in 1950 at the KNAF Studio. Courtesy of Mrs. Lorenz Schuch.

Walter Pehl fishing at the waterfall in Grape Creek in 1913. The waterfall was located just below his home in Luckenbach. Courtesy of Jeanette Klein.

All of the granddaughters gathered for a picture at the Fiftieth Wedding Anniversary in 1908 of Friedrich and Amalia Wilke. Courtesy of Margaret McCarn.

Local Bank Band. Courtesy of Darlene Stehle.

Sixteen-year-old William Lewis and his twelve-year-old brother, Leroy Lewis, pose with William's trophy shot at the Lewis ranch in 1948. Both boys were born on the Lewis Ranch. Courtesy of William Lewis

The Masken Ball was first hosted by the Casino Club in the Nimitz Hotel in the late 1800s. This celebration which occurred prior to Lent served as final "fling" before the traditional Lenten Fasting took place. The Gillespie County Historical Society revived the tradition again in the 1960s. The annual ball still takes place each year as a fundraiser for the Historical Society. This photo taken in 1976 shows the "Most Spirited" group award in 1976. Courtesy of Mrs. Milton Petermann.

Hunting has been many things in Gillespie County, a necessity, a revenue generator for ranchers, and a means of entertainment. These seven men gathered for a hunting trip circa 1910. Jake Krueger, unknown, Felix Reinbach, Henry W. Braeutigam, unknown, Otto Henke, and Rudolph Mueller. Courtesy of Carolyn Montgomery.

The famous Hoeltzer Band was organized in 1905 and played together for nearly fourteen years. The leader of the band, William Hoeltzer, was from Luckenbach. He was a strict band leader, perhaps due to his military training. This disciplined leadership enabled the band to become one of the finest rural bands in the nation during its time. Courtesy of Stonewall Heritage Society.

The Tatsch family poses by a picnic table donated by the children of Peter Tatsch and Conradina Ernst Tatsch. The park is located on the former Peter Tatsch place and the old Tatsch home now serves as a clubhouse in Lady Bird Johnson Park in Fredericksburg. Pictured are Hilda Kott, Viola Marschall, Dina Schaper, Lina Ahrens, Belton Tatsch, Ferdinand Tatsch, Charlie Eckstein, Edmund Tatsch, Emil Tatsch, and Reinhold Tatsch. Photographed in 1914, courtesy of Mrs. Leroy Rode.

Alvin Weinheimer (right) and companion display the bounty of their hunt—squirrels! Circa 1928. Courtesy of Stonewall Heritage Society.

These men shared part of their meal with their hunting hounds circa 1919. Courtesy of Stonewall Heritage Society.

These men posed circa 1900 with their prize buck, proving that hunting pictures in Gillespie County go about as far back as the camera. Courtesy of Stonewall Heritage Society.

William Dietel Jr. was the first Red Cross Certified swimming instructor in the county. This photo was taken at the Fredericksburg Tourist Park in 1936. The park, which was located on Goehmann Lane, consisted of a swimming pool, a nine-hole golf course, and cabins. Later Dr. Feller bought the property and today much of it remains in his family. Courtesy of Mr. Fred Dietel.

Local girl scouts get a tour of the inside of the Fredericksburg Radio Post in 1957. Pictured from left to right are: Vernell Walters, Vicki Loudon, Linda Krauskopf, Judy Friedrich, Lynette Crenwelge, Peggy Landis, Cheryl Feuge, Earline Webb, Erna Dietel Heinen. Second row, Sylvia Evers, Carol Pittman, Hermina Krauskopf, and Otelia Walters. Courtesy of Linda Langerhans.

Quilting was a popular pastime for women in the community. Hard work, artistry, and companionship were combined to make keepsakes that are now treasured. These women met in the basement of Holy Ghost Lutheran Church. Courtesy of Holy Ghost Lutheran Church.

Balanced Rock was a favorite spot for boys to take their favorite girls during the 1920s. The rock, located on private property, was intriguing to all. Unfortunately, immediately prior to the county's 125-year celebration the rock tumbled down from its resting place of many years. Whether the incident was simply an act of nature or an intentional act of destruction remains unknown. Courtesy of Ken Crenwelge.

E. H. Riley (far left) hosts a polo match at his ranch on Tivydale Road circa 1920. Polo was a popular pastime in the county until the 1930s. Dr. Felix Keidel, a local dentist, broke his neck in a fall, permanently dampening area enthusiasm for the sport. Courtesy of Melissa Starry.

Peter's Bar, located on the corner of West Main and North Orange of Fredericksburg, was at one time a hub of social activity in the community. Part of the building functioned as a confectionery known for their five-cent cherry cokes. The rest of the building was used for a variety of purposes over the years. At one time there was a restaurant within the building and between the bar and the confectionery was an area that later became a liquor store. The building also housed a large dance hall, Peter's Opera House and Dance Hall. A small room was provided for young families to bed down their small children on cots and pallets so the parents could enjoy dancing. The dance hall had a large stage across the back and high school graduations, Saengerfest, wedding receptions, and many other special occasion were celebrated there. On Saturdays there were even movies shown at Peter's Hall. Courtesy of the *Standard*.

The Fredericksburg Giants Baseball team late 1920s. Courtesy of Ken Crenwelge.

It has been said that stories about Enchanted Rock traveled all the way to Germany reaching the ears of Ottfried von Meusebach. Meusebach was enthusiastic to see the large rock and discover why it creaked and popped in the night. The Indians also had a fascination with the large rock, often making human sacrifices on it to appease the bad spirit they thought made its home there. These types of thoughts seem far removed from the Keidel brothers and their wives as they enjoy Enchanted Rock in the early 1900s. Courtesy of RoShell Baker.

Often the community's social life was intertwined with the church. Four members of Holy Ghost Lutheran Church Brotherhood prepare for a convention in Colorado. From left to right: Alex Frantzen, Edger Stroeher, Dr. Lorence Feller, and Benno Eckert Sr. all bought hats and boots to be Texas cowboys. Courtesy of Holy Ghost Lutheran.

The Fredericksburg Concert band played every year all three days at the fair, for all the parades, and any other big event in the county. Courtesy of Adele Pfiester Duecker.

Luckenbach, Texas, was founded in 1849. Guich Koock and Hondo Crouch purchased the town in 1974 and gave it flair. They staged events that drew huge crowds and national attention. In 1977 Waylon Jennings recorded "Let's Go to Luckenbach, Texas," the biggest hit single of the year. Courtesy of Mrs. J. Hardin Perry.

As the community became more established, more time could be spent in leisure. The women on this float, at the fiftieth anniversary of Fredericksburg in 1896, represent a local *kaffe klatsch*. At a kaffe klatsch, the hostess prepared lavish and elaborate desserts and her guests came dressed in their finest. The women discussed the issues of the day, and probably did a fair share of gossiping. This continued for years as the women tested one another's hostessing skills. From the left are: Alvina Gold, Anna Gold, Lula Lingsweiler, Mrs. Albert Detjen, Ella Stucken, Ida Beckman, Mrs. Ebbie Schmidt, Olga Hagen, Miss Beckman, Annie Blum, and Elise Henke Kiehne. Courtesy of Mrs. Wesley Gold.

In 1886 the Casino Club was formed with thirty members. Within ten years membership reached 120. The Casino Club staged dramatic and elaborate productions and sponsored masquerade balls and dances at the Nimitz Hotel. Members danced quadrilles, polkas, schottisches, and waltzes. The occasion came to a close as the lamps began to flicker. Lamps were filled with oil only once. A masquerade ball was held prior to Lent so members could have a final fling before the Lenten season. This tradition was revived by the Gillespie County Historical Society in 1960s in the form of the Masken Ball. Courtesy of the Gillespie County Historical Society.

Weddings in Gillespie County have always been an occasion for celebration. The church ceremony was generally followed by a meal and a dance. Due to the closeness of the community, often a general invitation was placed in the paper to avoid overlooking any potential well wisher. The bride and groom often were married on the twenty-fifth anniversary of one set of their parents. Sometimes this was also the grandparents' anniversary. On February 20, 1917, Alfred C. Metzger and Alma Stehling were married. Also pictured from left to right are: Alla A. Metzger, Max C. Stehling, Alfred C. Metzger, Alma Marie _____, Max Kunz, Cecilia Stehling, Max Schmidtzinsky, and Charlotte Stehling. Courtesy of Reuben and Margaret Kammlah.

Chapter Six

Modes of Transportation

"The first automobile around Stonewall, a 1906 model Ford, was bought by August Hahne.

"Whenever he met a horse-team, he had to stop and get out of the car to help the horse get by. Finally the horses got used to the car."

—*100 Years*, Otto Lindig

Opposite page: After landing at the old fairgrounds for refueling, this barnstormer took off toward the bright blue yonder. Unfortunately, he did not gain enough altitude and found his plane entangled in power lines thirty feet above the ground. The pilot was not injured and the plane did not burn. Not surprisingly, this pilot's flight became famous in "Ripley's Believe It or Not." Courtesy of Fred Dietel.

Alvin H. Weinheimer and a friend get around in a faster fashion with their new bicycles in the early 1900s. Courtesy of the Stonewall Heritage Society.

Edgar Stroeher (right), founder of Stroeher & Son, Inc., makes a gas delivery in the 1920s to the South Heights Station on 710 East Main. The gasoline was delivered in ten-gallon milk cans. On the left is Anton Jenschke. Courtesy of Roy Stroeher.

In the early years of Gillespie County the ox cart was an invaluable mode of hauling goods from place to place. This photo was taken on Main Street. In the far right stands a bar which later became Security State Bank. Further to the left is the courthouse, present day Pioneer Memorial Library. Courtesy of the *Standard*.

The first Fredericksburg fire truck was not operated by a mega horsepower engine, but rather might and manpower. This photo was taken at the site of the modern fire station around 1912. Today the volunteer fire departments of all the communities in the county are an integral and essential part of protecting Gillespie County residents. Courtesy of the Stonewall Heritage Society.

Although our mode of transportation has changed over time, one thing remains the same, children all still love a wagon. Elmer Luckenbach and Weston J. Luckenbach pose for this picture circa 1925. Courtesy of Roscoe Basse.

Few people know that the infamous Elephant Saloon once served as a gas station in the late 1920s. Gas was fifteen cents for regular and seventeen cents for supreme. Gus Brauer (back to camera) was the owner of what was called Brauer Auto Supply. Courtesy of Roy Stroeher.

In this photo county commissioners inspect the new roller and grader. Gillespie County has seen marked improvements under the leadership of dedicated commissioners. Courtesy of Linda Langerhans.

The Max T. Henke Store and Station served as the county's first "convenience store." The business began in the 1920s and enabled shoppers to purchase groceries, school supplies, gasoline, and beer all in one place—a real novelty in the 1920s. The store was located on the corner of Travis and Llano Street close to the college building, the only school in town at the time. Students and adults alike enjoyed sipping a soda or visiting with friends at the Henke store. Courtesy of Hans and Dorothy Hannemann.

Before the advent of supermarkets and department stores, people had to go to specialty shops for various items. Because this could prove time consuming, some businesses provided delivery services. Henke Meat Market was such a business and employed Udo Henke, Richard Henke's son, as a delivery boy. Udo was a mere five years old when this picture was taken of him on his trusty steed making deliveries. Photo taken in 1910, courtesy of RoShell Henke Baker.

This wagon was used by the owners of the lumber mill next to the Kuenemann house pictured. The drivers of the wagon used it to deliver milled wood to building sites. Courtesy of Paul Hamilton.

Edgar Stroeher, Charles Dolezal, and Reinhold Eckhardt enjoy a break from work while filling up a gas truck. Edger Stroeher, founder of Stroeher & Son, Inc., purchased the agency from Eckhardt in 1930 for one thousand dollars. The business prospered and remains in the family today. The present day Stroeher and Son building is located at 509 South Adams Street. Courtesy of Roy Stroeher.

This ox train was the type that was used to transport goods and people from New Braunfels to Fredericksburg when the town first originated. Courtesy of the Stonewall Heritage Society.

Top: Gone were the horse and buggy days by the early 1900s. This photo taken on Creek Street shows the cars lining the street as people gathered for the Staatsverband Convention. Courtesy of Corrine Danysh.

Bottom: After years of hard work and disappointment, the community was thrilled when the day finally came for the train to come to town. In honor of the event a parade and four days' worth of celebration was organized. The Railroad Committee and the Fredericksburg Progressive League had the honor of having their own float in the parade. Seated in the back row with a bowler hat is Temple Smith, the man whose efforts were largely responsible for the final arrival of the train. Courtesy of the *Standard*.

Everyone put on their Sunday best and rode to town in their horse and buggy to see the new train. One farmer was said to have walked over to the train, patted it and said, "Poor thing. You must be very tired." Courtesy of the *Standard*.

It took hard work and strong backs to lay the track for the Fredericksburg and Northern Railroad. Progress took time and was greatly slowed when the men reached the hill where the tunnel was to be placed. Work was carried on around the clock with three shifts taking turns attempting to bore a hole through the stubborn terrain. Today that tunnel is home to well over a million bats. A historical marker has been placed there and tourists come from miles around to see the bats ascend to the sky in the evenings. Courtesy of Roscoe Basse.

Henry Alberthal, William Thiele, and Edmund Alberthal working immediately after World War I in Blanchard's Vulcanizing Shop. The shop was located on Main Street near Llano Street. Courtesy of Norman and Mildred Wilke.

This photo shows one of the first automobiles in the county. It was owned by Sam E. Johnson, father of Lyndon Baines Johnson. Young Lyndon is standing directly in front of the car. Years later, Henry Ford, while visiting Lyndon and his wife, Lady Bird, at their ranch in Stonewall, was moved by this photograph. So moved was Ford that he sent another Model T from Dearborn, Michigan. Ford's gift now stands on the first floor of the LBJ Library in Austin. Courtesy of Mrs. Lyndon Baines Johnson (Lady Bird).

This photo was taken in front of the old college building circa 1905. Miss Julia Estill is seated in the third row, third from right. Estill, a dedicated teacher, taught for years in the Fredericksburg school. Courtesy of Eugene Sidlo.

Chapter Seven

The Three R's

In 1847 the first school in Gillespie County began in Fredericksburg in the newly constructed Vereins Kirche. Tuition was one dollar per pupil, per quarter. Attendance was irregular due to the disease and hardship that wreaked havoc on the community's families. To help the teacher supplement his income, school was conducted only in the morning, enabling the teacher to engage in afternoon money making ventures. However, the community's first schoolteacher, Johann Leyendecker, needing to provide for his large family, left his post and sought a more consistent source of income.

The next teacher at the new school was Jacob Brodbeck, a man who wanted to invent a "flying ship." After his teaching stint, Brodbeck was followed by the Reverend Burchard Dangers. Dangers carried the double duty of pastoring and teaching until he was relieved by Heinrich Ochs. *Lehrer* (teacher) Ochs toiled for four years within the octagonal walls of the Vereins Kirche, teaching sixty to seventy pupils at a time. The unusual building lacked tight walls, a tight roof, and solid flooring. The students sat on crude, backless, oak benches and went through the school day with virtually no supplies. Teaching and learning in the new frontier was clearly a labor of love.

The students learned and the teachers taught under these conditions until 1854, a landmark year for Texas education. Until that time local communities organized schools and financed them through student tuition. That year, however, the Texas state legislature established a public school system. Out of one hundred counties in Texas only two or three took the

During the early years children received an education in a variety of places. One of Fredericksburg's first teachers, Christian Kraus, taught lessons in this log home. Several students attended for many years. Courtesy of Trudy Kraus.

opportunity to create school districts. Gillespie County, on the other hand, created *five* school districts. Many of the settlers in Gillespie County had received a fine education in Europe and wanted their children to be educated in a similar fashion. Furthermore, through the new legislative act, teachers received a steady income if they taught the English language in the local school. Therefore, instructors' financial duress somewhat waned. That same year marked the opening of the first public school in Gillespie County and the county's first parochial school, St. Mary's.

The trustees elected August Siemering as the first schoolmaster of the public school in 1856. Siemering moved to Fredericksburg from Sisterdale where he served as secretary for the Latin community, a group of intellectual idealists. Siemering, a highly educated man and an able writer, also worked as a journalist, again to supplement his income. Siemering's dual duties were demanding, consequently a second teacher was sought. Franz Stein filled the position and the two worked together until the Civil War when Siemering left his teaching post and joined the Union army. Unfortunately, his replacement, Louis Schuetze, also a Union sympathizer, fell prey to the menacing *Haengerbande* (hanging gang), a group of roving thugs which targeted Union sympathizers. During the volatile Civil War period many of the rural schools curtailed or ceased classes.

Once the Civil War was over, school resumed and several communities established new rural schools, often on land that was donated by local citizens. Country schoolchildren rode their horses or walked as far as seven miles to attend class where school amenities were rather sparse. Many rurals schools didn't even have a water well, forcing students and the teacher to depend on the hospitality of neighbors. When illness ran rampant through the community the students brought their own cup rather than share the same dipper.

Throughout their existence most rural schools, like their counterparts in town, charged tuition to operate the schools. Teachers adapted school schedules in order for children to help their parents during harvest time. However, not all children in Gillespie County were able to attend school. Some were taught at home by their mothers and attended school sporadically, only when it was convenient to do so. "I was more than fifteen years old before I ever attended school. My mother had given us all the help she could, and we had applied ourselves to studying such books as we had. " (Biggers, p. 85)

The end of each school year was marked by the *Schulpruefung* (school examination), an all day affair. The

Students pose in front of Weinheimer Hall in Stonewall in 1945 as they get ready for their blessed school closing. In the top row from left to right are: William Brandenburger, Alton Klier, George Vogel, and Ruben Wehmeyer. In the bottom row are: Martin Meier and Herbert Immel. Courtesy of Nelda Vogel.

After the Catholic School began in the home of the priest, it was soon moved to a piece of property known as the Straube House on the north corner of West San Antonio and South Milam Streets. Courtesy of Trudy Kraus.

The Cherry Mountain school was organized in 1883 and had ten students. Initially the school taught only five grades but later expanded to eighth grade. Occasionally the school building was lit by gasoline lanterns, and night classes were held for the eighth and ninth grades. Schoolchildren pose in front of the school in 1925. Courtesy of Mrs. Lorenz Schuch.

students dressed in their best clothes and demonstrated their accomplishments to parents and guests. To accommodate guests an arbor was generally constructed. Once the guests arrived each class took an oral exam over the material they learned that year. The exam closed with a program given by the students followed by a picnic with beer, good food, and music. Then the school room was cleared and dancing festivities began. This tradition continued well into the latter part of the nineteenth century.

Further demonstrating the priority placed on education in the community, the German Methodist Church spearheaded an effort to establish a college in Fredericksburg. The church raised money through voluntary community contributions. A building was erected on what came to be known as College Hill. Present day College Street runs past the building which is still standing and is currently a part of the middle school campus.

In 1876, the college received its first students. Out of town students lived in the upper level, and the principal and his wife served as supervisors. However, the majority of students were Fredericksburg residents. Some young men and women were quite eager to further their education, walking as far as five miles morning and night to attend the college. One of these dedicated students, C. W. Feuge, later served as superintendent of the Frederickburg school for sixteen years.

After nine years of educating students the college could no longer operate. Inadequate funds forced its closing, and the college was sold in 1884 to the Fredericksburg Independent School District. The building was then used as the sole school building for the Fredericksburg public school. The building housed grades one through nine for ten years until the growth in student numbers demanded that more rooms be added. As time progressed various school principals attempted to persuade the community to add more grades, and in due time, they did.

In the early 1900s minutes began being taken on school business. The minutes recorded such information as teacher pay: in 1907, two lady assistant teachers received forty dollars per month and two men received sixty dollars per month. The minutes also recorded controversy—such as the teacher who in 1924 was asked to resign for taking an "active part in a style show." She modeled a "modern" swimsuit—questionable behavior for a schoolteacher at that time.

The first school graduation exercises were held at Klaerners Opera House. The lower grades delivered drills and recitations, and the upper grades performed plays in English and in German. The first Baccalaureate was held in 1918, at the Southern Methodist Church. The service was conducted by Zion Lutheran pastor, Rev. F. A. Bracher.

The community continued to grow, and so did the need for more space for the students. One by one the small rural schools consolidated into the Fredericksburg School District. Buildings were added to the central campus on College Hill to accommodate growth, but by the 1960s, the school could no longer be maintained on the central campus.

Today the Fredericksburg Independent School District has four separate campuses in Fredericksburg where children

If walls could tell tales, this building would surely write books. It has been used over one hundred years for educating the people of Gillespie County. The building first served as a college and later as the sole school building for the Fredericksburg school. Today it is still in use as part of the Middle School campus. The student body was photographed in 1876. Courtesy of the *Standard*.

The only school in the county for colored children was built through private donations from the community. The black population was quite small in the county and often there were as few as five students enrolled in the school. The building has been moved, but is still in existence and presently serves as a guest house. Courtesy of the *Standard*.

The first lessons were taught in the Grapetown school in 1859 by Louise Hartwig, a native of Scotland. Classes were canceled during the Civil War and then resumed on land donated by Friedrich Baag. The gift of land came with the stipulation that no religious or political meetings would take place on the property. In 1944 the school consolidated with the Cain City School. Courtesy of the Stonewall Heritage Society.

through the twelfth grade attend. The Harper school also educates children through the twelfth grade, while the Stonewall school educates children through the fifth grade. Doss schools educate children through the eighth grade. Adding to the public schools in the county are the preparatory, parochial, and Protestant Christian schools. Additionally, some families in the county educate their children in similar fashion to the original settlers through home-schooling.

Education in the county changed with each class. Today's Gillespie County students no longer sit on crude, backless oak benches, but have access to fine facilities and the latest technology. One thing, however, remains the same—providing a good education for the young people of Gillespie County.

When the first Crabapple School was built there was a difference of opinion regarding where the school should be located. To resolve the conflict, two men, Conrad Welgehausen and Crocket Riley, agreed to run a foot race. Conrad Welgehausen won and was well rewarded for his speed. The school was built less than a mile from his home. Crabapple schoolchildren pose in front of the Vereins Kirche in Fredericksburg. Courtesy of Geraldine Dittmar.

Jacob Brodbeck may have been one of Fredericksburg's most interesting teachers. It is said that Brodbeck studied the seagulls as he sailed from Germany to America. While watching them he became certain that there must be a better way to travel other than by ship.

Brodbeck arrived in Fredericksburg in 1847 and took over the teacherage from Johann Leyendecker. Although he had his hands full teaching and starting a new life, Brodbeck was an inventor at heart, and many of his inventions were fascinating to the townspeople. Still, his dream of a flying machine was dismissed as fantasy. Undaunted, Brodbeck pursued the dream and succeeded, be it ever so briefly. In 1865 he completed his "flying ship." With a crowd looking on the machine soared into the sky and then crashed to the ground. Brodbeck, who had been flying the machine, was injured in the crash. Worse than the physical injury was the fact that his supporters had completely lost confidence in the project. Six years before Brodbeck died the Wright brothers flew at Kitty Hawk. Courtesy of Harry Keller.

In 1858 people in the area began teaching children in their homes. Lehrer Ochs traveled to the community and taught in three different families' homes for two days in each. The community desired to build a school, but their hopes were snuffed out by the onset of the Civil War. Only after the war had ended were they able to build a schoolhouse. In 1869 children of the Washingtons, freed slaves, attended school with the Anglo children. This was probably one of the first integrated schools in the South. The school still stands at Meusebach Creek. Courtesy of the Stonewall Heritage Society.

Live Oak School circa 1895. The teacher is thought to be a Mr. Fischer. Courtesy of Jeanette Koger.

This school was the second built in District No. 33. It was called the Lindemann School because the Lindemann family had the most children in the school. This building, no longer standing, was replaced by a third building that is still used for community events. Courtesy of the Stonewall Heritage Society.

The first Rheingold school was built in 1873. Within the town lived two widows of two brothers, Jacob and Peter Gold, both of whom succumbed to the harsh conditions in Indianola. The widows had six sons between them, all with the last name of Gold. Consequently the community came to be known as Rheingold meaning "pure gold." Students rode horses to school and, when it rained, placed their saddles under the porch. In 1949 the school consolidated with Fredericksburg. Courtesy of the Stonewall Heritage Society.

Left: One of the first Catholic schoolteachers, Christian Kraus, arrived in America in 1851. After attempting to make his living at cigar making, he headed west from New York. He eventually ended his travels in Fredericksburg where he was reunited with his former teacher, Johann Leyendecker, founder of the first school in Fredericksburg. Kraus taught in the Catholic school, taught private lessons in a log cabin, and also taught in the public school located on "Marktplatz." Courtesy of Trudy Kraus.

Nuns pose with some of the first students at St. Mary's school in Fredericksburg. St. Mary's began in 1856 with seven students being taught in the priest's house. The little school had a successful year and by 1857, attendance was up to forty-seven. Unfortunately the following fall, due to crop failure, the school was forced to close its doors. Happily it reopened in 1858. Today St. Mary's continues to educate children in Gillespie County. Courtesy of Trudy Kraus.

In 1885, through a combined community effort, the Rocky Hill School was erected without any aid from the state. Located on Highway 290 east of Fredericksburg, the school building was constructed for $196.02. The need for student transportation arose when the school consolidated with Grapetown and Cain City in the 1950s. When the need was met though, the arrival of the new school bus meant added responsibility for the teacher—as bus driver. This photo shows the children standing in front of the new bus. In 1977 the school finally closed its doors. It has been used in recent years as a restaurant. Courtesy of the Stonewall Heritage Society.

The Albert School began as a stone building. Later a pressed tin room was added. Interestingly, Lyndon B. Johnson received one year of his education in this school. Courtesy of the Stonewall Heritage Society.

At the Stonewall School during the early 1930s. In the back row from left to right are: Martin Bauer, Emil Deike, Werner Burg, Kermit Hahne, Eddie Ellebracht, Ruben Ellebracht, and Paul Wallendorf. In the front row are: Edgar Leonard, Rubin Ottmers, Herbert Haas (teacher), Tille Ahrens, Tom Weinheimer, and Alois Nebgen. Tillie Ahrens, the only girl in the class, later married Kermit Hahne. Courtesy of the Stonewall Heritage Society.

In 1876 Willow City's first school was built. The structure pictured was built in 1905, of native rock. There were three rooms with the upstairs serving as an auditorium in the early years. Later the upstairs served as a classroom. Willow City was not reputed to be a sleepy little village. It had been infiltrated by a few bad characters who gave the little town a poor reputation. Consequently, the school had its share of trouble. On one occasion the teacher had to forcefully remove a six-shooter from a student. It was not uncommon for knives to appear during playground fights, and upon one occasion, a boy about twelve years of age lost his life from a knife wound he received at school. In later years this bad influence was alleviated, and the school became a calmer place of learning. Courtesy of the Stonewall Heritage Society.

"Our feet were tough as a horse's hoofs. We could kick a fire out of flint rock, figuratively speaking. We could skate all day on the ice, without shoes and with only a short shirt of thin cloth, and not suffer from the cold." So said Bernhard Fiedler in an interview in 1925. This was the case with many children during this time frame. The boys from the Williams Creek School located at Albert appear to be a hearty bunch with and without shoes. The first Albert School was built out of logs and later replaced with this stone building. Photo taken circa 1900, courtesy of the Stonewall Heritage Society.

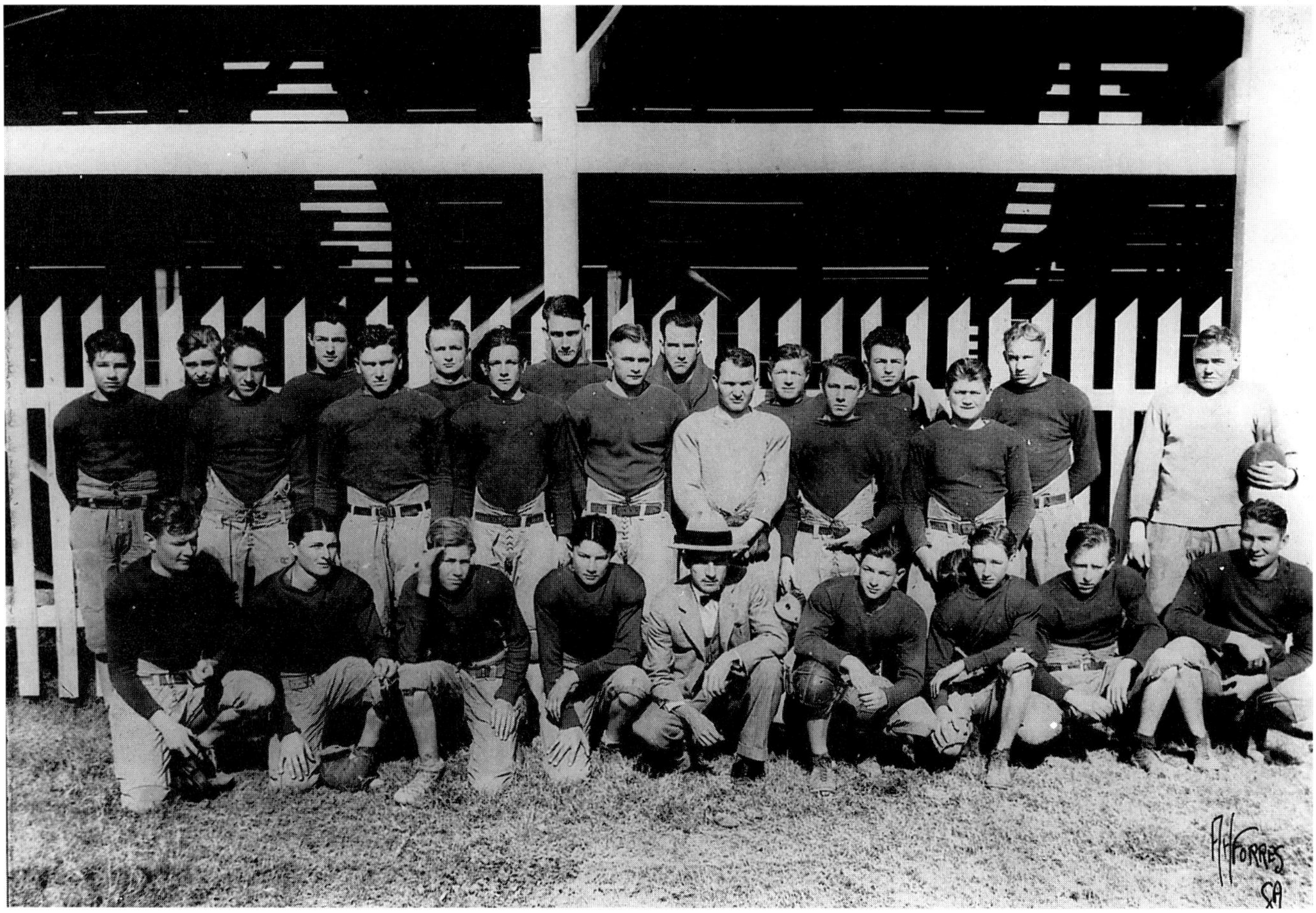

Fredericksburg High School Football team 1928. Courtesy of Mary Louise Sidlo.

The Morris School House was designed by architect Alfred Giles, the same architect who designed the second courthouse. Today the building serves as a residence. Courtesy of the *Standard*.

Doss schoolgirls walked many miles in order to get to school. Courtesy of Edna Crenwelge, a retired Doss school teacher who taught for many years.

These 1924 Doss schoolchildren often rode horses as far as five miles into school. The Doss school, though one of the smaller public schools in the county, is the pride of the Doss community. Courtesy of Edna Crenwelge.

Doss schoolchildren gather at a scrap metal pile gathered for the World War II effort. Courtesy of Sherrie Geistweidt.

Ella Gold (center) was one of Fredericksburg's talented and dedicated teachers. She also helped author *Pioneers in Gods Hills* and assisted the Junior Historians. Her knowledge of the county and her teaching abilities were widely respected. Also in photo are Carolyn Vogel on the left and Carol Beckmann to the right. Photograph taken in 1971, courtesy of the *Standard*.

Fredericksburg public school's 1925 football team. These handsome young men played football with no helmets, no face masks, but plenty of rugged, raw courage. Courtesy of Dr. John Walch.

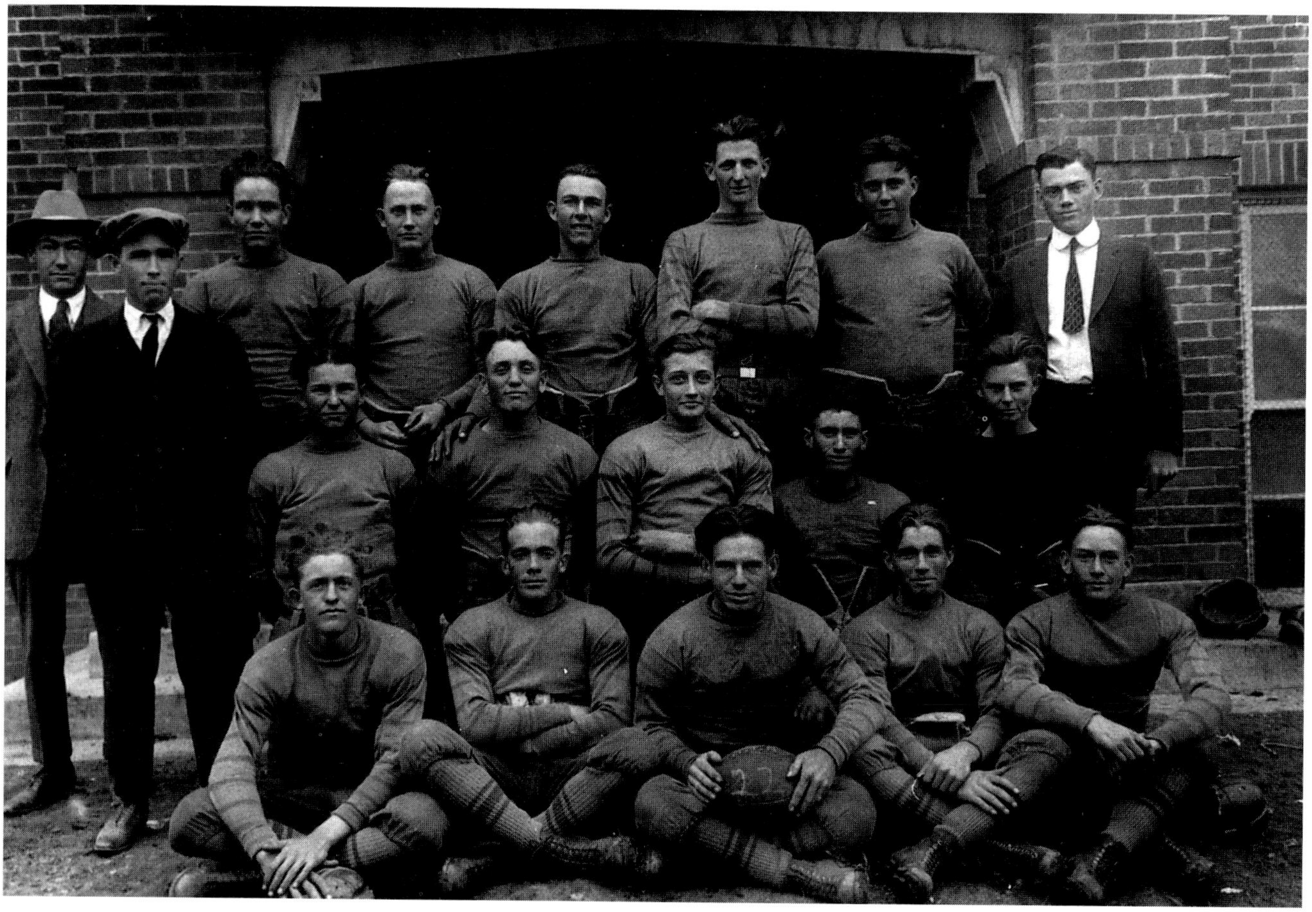

This 1926 classroom photograph depicts the fanciful days before the long years of the Depression. Note the cast iron sides of the student's desks. Courtesy of Dr. John Walch.

The Lady Billies basketball team advanced to the state tournament 1994-95. The girls basketball team has been strong over the years, advancing to playoffs twelve of the thirteen years that Don Brookshire has been their coach. Past teams to advance to the state tournament were the 1947, 1948, 1951, and 1985 teams. Courtesy of Fredericksburg High School.

Opposite top: In the 1920s Mrs. F. J. Maier organized a kindergarten and conducted classes in her home. Twenty-two years later Elsie Lochte took over the kindergarten. Lochte's kindergarten class of 1955 class performs their end of the year program. Courtesy of Betty Green.

Opposite bottom: After the program, students dressed up to receive their diplomas. Courtesy of Betty Green.

Doss girls basketball team, 1933. Courtesy of Edna Crenwelge.

Top: The new high school was built in 1964 and continues to be utilized as the main building of the high school campus. Courtesy of the *Standard*.

Concentration and determination mark the percussion section of the Fredericksburg 1993 Marching Band. The Fredericksburg Marching Band has a long standing tradition of being top quality and received high honors on many occasions. Courtesy of the *Standard*.

The following list of rural schools was compiled from the Gillespie County Courthouse records. All names appear as they were found in court records.

Big Flat	Morris Ranch
Bear Creek	Nebgen
Cain City	Nebo (Eckert)
Cave Creek	Onion Creek
Cherry Mountain	Palo Alto
Cherrie Springs	Pecan Creek
Crab Apple	Pedernales
Doss	Petersburg
Flat Rock	Pilot Knob
Grape Creek (Lower South)	Pocket
Grapetown	Rheingold
Grape Hill	Rocky Hill
Hayden	Stonewall
Honey Creek	Squaw Creek
Junction	Tiveydale
Klein Branch	Young's Chapel
Klein Frankreich	White Oak
Knopp	Williams Creek (Albert)
Live Oak	Willow City
Luckenbach	Wolf Creek
Meusebach Creek	Wrede

The Harper School was established in 1884. The original schoolhouse burned down, but part of the second school building was incorporated into the school shown here which was built in 1940. Courtesy of the Harper Historical Society.

The local PTA has a long standing tradition of contributing to the education of the young people in Gillespie County. These ladies pose in 1956 depicting the various periods of the PTA. From left to right are: Emily Schmidt, Ollie Wells, Florine Feller, Faye Henke, Louise Dietel, and May Cox. The PTA cookbook which is still in demand has helped financed many special projects sponsored by the organization. Courtesy of the Fredericksburg PTA.

Chapter Eight

Those of Influence

"... The United States is the average person, who, like yourself, is living as an individual proud of his liberties, conscious of his responsibility to his neighbor, participating in his government, self-disciplined by education, and, by education inspired to further God's will on earth."

—Admiral Chester Nimitz

Although the annals of Gillespie County were written primarily by the average person, the undaunted unknown, there have also been those sons of Gillespie County that made lasting impressions on the United States and world history pages. These notable figures have made the citizens of Gillespie County proud as they have represented the deepest desire in all of us to make the world a better place.

Left: Emil Sauer was born in 1881 in the original house of the Sauer Beckmann Homestead in Stonewall's LBJ Park. From such humble beginnings, Sauer went on to receive his education at the University of Texas and Harvard. In 1910 he was a special agent of the U.S. Census Bureau and then examiner of the U.S. Tariff Board. Sauer then served as consul in seven foreign countries. He also penned several books on finance, loans, and investments. Pictured are Sauer and his bride Victoria Vale Sauer in 1919. Courtesy of Dora Stein.

Frank Valentin van der Stucken was born in 1858 in Fredericksburg, Texas. At an early age he was taken to Belgium where he studied music. A talented composer, van der Stucken went on to make his mark on music worldwide. He was the first to conduct Brahms' *Third Symphony* in the United States and also conducted the first European concert which contained music composed only by Americans. Courtesy of Betsy Delforge.

Lady Bird, or Bird for short, attended college at the University of Texas in Austin where she met the young Lyndon Johnson. After a whirlwind romance which lasted all of two months, the two were married and embarked on the journey of a lifetime together. Lady Bird helped finance his first campaign which made him a member of the House of Representatives. When Lyndon fought in World War II, Lady Bird took over his staff and fielded questions and concerns from his constituents. Some of her own favorite projects, those dealing with conservation and beautification, remain her favorite. Although she makes her permanent home in Austin, Lady Bird has remained a friend and contributor to Gillespie County. Courtesy of the Stonewall Heritage Society.

Lieutenant Louis Jordan was the first Texas casualty in World War I. He died in France, on March 5, 1918. While attending the University of Texas he led its football team to their first undefeated season as the captain of the team. He was also the first Southwest Conference football player to be named on an All American football team. Courtesy of the Gillespie County Historical Society.

Gerald Harvey Jones, known as G. Harvey, one of the most famous living American artists, lives and paints in Fredericksburg. He was born in Kerrville, and as a boy, often traveled to Fredericksburg with his father. His works have drawn national and international attention, and in 1991-1992 the Smithsonian Museum in Washington, D.C., featured his works in a one man exhibition focusing on the American horse. Courtesy of G. Harvey.

Charles Henry Nimitz established the Nimitz Hotel in 1860. The Nimitz family lived on the premises and provided comfortable lodging and delicious food for people traveling across the frontier. In the 1870s Nimitz expanded the hotel and added a steamboat-like facade. The hotel was used for Casino Club events and other social functions. In 1926 the hotel was sold and remodeled. In 1964 it became the Museum of the Pacific War. Admiral Nimitz agreed to allow the Museum to be named in his honor with the stipulation that it be dedicated to all the men and women who served in the armed forces. The museum was renovated and the steamboat facade was replaced. Courtesy of George Vogel.

The Nimitz Hotel after the "naval" addition. Courtesy of the *Standard*.

The Nimitz Museum as it appears in 1995. Courtesy of the *Standard*.

The modernization of the Nimitz Hotel. Courtesy of the *Standard*.

Born in Fredericksburg and raised by his grandfather Nimitz, Chester W. Nimitz was perhaps the greatest U.S. Navy's admiral in the twentieth century. After the bombing of Pearl Harbor, President Franklin D. Roosevelt named Chester Nimitz commander in chief of the Pacific Fleet. Nimitz commanded over six million men and women in the Pacific Campaign of World War II. After successfully orchestrating U.S. military might and forcing the surrender of Japan, Nimitz was hailed as a hero. Following the war he was honored in Washington, New York City, and then finally in his home town of Fredericksburg. Nimitz went on to be chief of Naval Operations and also served in the United Nations. Courtesy of the *Standard*.

In September 1995 past president George Bush Sr. once again visited Fredericksburg for the dedication of the George Bush Gallery of the Pacific War, and to celebrate the V+50 parade commemorating the end of World War II's Pacific Campaign. With Bush in the military vehicle is George Bush Jr. (left) presently the governor of Texas. They are riding down San Antonio Street in Fredericksburg. Courtesy of the *Standard*.

In 1993 ground breaking ceremonies were held in Fredericksburg for the George Bush Gallery of the Pacific War. Pictured from left to right are: Maggie and Gordon Sauer, John Benson, Barbara and George Bush, and Peggy Benson. Courtesy of the *Standard*.

The thirty-fourth president of the United States was born in Gillespie County on the ranch which is now a part of LBJ Park. Perhaps political life was in his blood as his father and grandfather had served in the Texas legislature. Johnson was first elected to public office in 1937 when he became a member of the House of Representatives. From that time on, Johnson's life was devoted to his constituents. Johnson was largely responsible for the addition of electricity in the rural communities as well as improving roads in the Hill Country. In 1951 he and Lady Bird bought a ranch from his aunt that had belonged to his grandparents. Together the Johnsons entertained friends and visiting dignitaries at what came to be known as the Texas Whitehouse. On January 22, 1973, the former president's life came full circle. He died at his beloved ranch, not far from the place where he was born. He was buried in the family cemetery in Stonewall, Texas, with the Rev. Dr. Billy Graham and Rev. Wunibald Schneider of Stonewall offering prayers.

President Lyndon Baines Johnson on the right and First Lady Lady Bird, and Stonewall's Simon Burg (center with glasses) admire a commemorative plate with Middle Eastern visitors at the Texas Whitehouse in Stonewall. Courtesy of the Stonewall Heritage Society.

Prior to Johnson's presidency, while he was yet a senator, German Chancellor Konrad Adenauer was honored at the LBJ Ranch on April 16, 1960. The third man on the left is retired Fleet Admiral Chester W. Nimitz. Courtesy of the *Standard*.

Chapter Nine

Fairs, Festivals, and Celebrations

Over the years many parades have made their way up and down Fredericksburg's Main Street. Parades have marked the climax to many events dear to the community's heart, such as the arrival of the railroad, Admiral Nimitz's homecoming, and the local fair. Early county parades ambled down the wide, dirt San Saba Street [Main Street], sporting elaborate horse-drawn floats. When Fredericksburg was fifty years old, a celebration to match all celebrations was staged. It was a three day affair, with fireworks, singing, concerts, bonfires, and of course, a parade. The grand celebration culminated with the lighting of strands of bulbs on the Vereins Kirche marking the introduction of electricity to Fredericksburg.

As time passed local organizations introduced new events that became a part of the culture and tradition of the county. Easter Fires, the Stonewall Peach Jamboree, Night in Old Fredericksburg, Kristkindl Markt, Fredericksburg's Food and Wine Fest, and Oktoberfest are just a few of the traditional events held annually in the county.

Opposite: Dr. Victor Keidel officiates as parade marshal for the 1946 Centennial Parade. Courtesy of Mrs. J. Hardin Perry.

This committee organized the celebration of the county's Fiftieth Anniversary. In the front row from left to right are: H. Ochs, L. Hagen, and E. Wahrmund. In the second row are: B. Blum, L. Patton, and Hermann Ochs. Courtesy of the *Standard.*

The centerpiece of the Fiftieth Anniversary celebration was the parade. The people created elaborate floats to represent various organizations and aspects of the colony's formation.

Float depicting a ship to the new world.

Below: View of Main Street during the parade.

Young girls dressed for the celebration enjoy the parade.

Elaborate details were the trademark of Fredericksburg's Fiftieth Anniversary Parade.

The two ladies on this float are dressed in costumes to represent the motherland, Germany, and the new land, America. Behind the float are brush arbors erected for the celebration. The walls of the Vereins Kirche were torn down and brush arbors built around the building. After the celebration the Vereins Kirche was torn down. Courtesy of Geraldine Dittmar.

Cinco de Mayo Celebration in Stonewall circa 1920s. The men in the front row are representatives from the Hierhoelzer Band. Courtesy of the Stonewall Heritage Society.

When the Seventy-fifth Anniversary rolled around, another committee was organized to officiate over the celebration. In the front row from left to right are: Lawrence Krauskopf, Henry Hirsch, Reverend A. Koerner, Judge Herman Usener, and Emil Kordzik. In the second row are: Richard Ludwig, Reverend Henry Gerlach, Reverend A. R. Vetter, and C. W. Feuge. In the back row are: William Dietel, Robert Blum, A. H. Kneese, Alfred Schmidt, and Emil Juenke. Courtesy of the Krauskopf Family.

The Seventy-fifth Anniversary Parade passed under a decorated frame representing the Vereins Kirche. Courtesy of Henry D. Kammlah.

162

The day the railroad finally came to town was a day for rejoicing. Although the happy crowd had to contend with poor weather, the celebration continued. Excited onlookers view "their" railroad. Courtesy of Geraldine Dittmar.

Seventy-fifth Anniversary Parade float. Courtesy of Kenneth Crenwelge.

From the left, Albert Moursund, Harry Gartrell, Emmie Patton Detjen, Cora Basse, August Gold, and Ebbie Schmidt all pose for a picture at the Seventy-fifth Anniversary Parade. Courtesy of the Krauskopf Family.

At the turn of the century, men and women considered the Fair a real event requiring their formal clothes. Courtesy of the *Standard*.

Men and women enjoyed the horse races at the turn of the century. For many years people from Morris Ranch walked their horses ten miles from the ranch west of the city to run in the races. Courtesy of the *Standard*.

A crowd gathered in 1935 for the dedication of the newly constructed Vereins Kirche replica. Courtesy of the *Standard*.

The Committee for the Centennial Celebration of 1946 included, in the front row from left to right: Robert Klingelhoefer, Lawrence Krauskopf, Miss Julia Estill, Mrs. Victor Keidel, William Petmecky, Mrs. Robert Blum, Mrs. Henry Lochte, Mayor Joe Molberg, and Max Reinbach. In the second row are: Arthur Kowert, William Dietel, Judge Henry Hirsch, Henry Houy, Alex Frantzen, Nolan Brown, and Alfred Neffendorf. Courtesy of the *Standard*.

These men depict the first settlers in the One Hundredth Anniversary Parade. Courtesy of the *Standard*.

Holy Ghost Lutheran creates a float to represent the first church services which were held outside under the oak trees. Courtesy of Ruben Wahrmund.

The Knopp and Metzger float for the One Hundredth Anniversary Celebration. Seated from left to right are: Bob, Tilda, and Fritz Metzger. The girls are: Genivieve Petsch, Virginia Heep, Kathleen Petsch, and Florine Enderlin. Courtesy of Fritz Metzger.

Lady Bird Johnson helps Stonewall celebrate its One Hundredth Anniversary as she rides atop the stagecoach in 1960. Courtesy of the Stonewall Heritage Society.

While the brave men of Fredericksburg were off attempting to meet with the Indians, the settlers were left behind in a somewhat precarious position. Likewise, the Indians felt vulnerable to attack. The Indians surrounded the town and burned large fires which were visible from the town. It is said that one mother calmed her children by telling them that the fires were built by Easter rabbits who were boiling large cauldrons of water to be used for cooking and decorating Easter eggs. This fabled story has become the center piece for the traditional Easter Fire Pageant. Occurring each year on Easter weekend, area children participate in the telling of the history of the founding of Fredericksburg. Here local Boy Scouts haul tires to the top of Cross Mountain to be burned in the fires. Courtesy of the *Standard*.

Harper residents portray first settlers in the June 1963 Centennial celebration. On the ground from the left are: Eldred Roach, Douglas Tatsch, and Elbert Feller. On the wagon are: Myrtle Feller, Nancy Feller, Sarah Lange, and Craig Lange. Courtesy of the Harper Historical Society.

Stonewall celebrates its 125th Anniversary in 1985 at the Peach Jamboree parade. Seated from left to right are: DeAnn Weinheimer, Karen Arizola, Luana Gold, and Suzanne Hartmann. Courtesy of the *Standard*.

Local residents enjoy a good time at the Oktoberfest in 1983. The festival has grown over the years and draws many tourists into Fredericksburg annually. Courtesy of the *Standard*.

The 125th Anniversary Committee included, in the front row from left to right: Robert W. Klingelhoefer, Mrs. J. Hardin Perry, Walter Edwards, Alex Frantzen, Mrs. Erna Dietel Heinen, and William M. Petmecky. In the second row are: Alois Jenschke, Perry Woerner, Hector Pedregon, Felix Stehling, Fred Mathisen, Gerald Schmidt, and Elgin Heimann. In the third row are: Mayor Sidney Henke, Arthur H. Kowert, Norman Rech, Belton Klinksiek, County Judge Victor H. Sagebiel, and Wallace Ottmers. Bert Warner is not pictured.

Men in each community all over the county formed shooting clubs. The men practiced together, honed their skills, and then gathered together at Grapetown for the original Schützenfest to determine who was the premier marksman. This tradition continues today. Photo circa 1885, courtesy of Kurt Kallenberg.

At the 1994 Founders Day celebration reenactment of the signing of the treaty, Larry Liles represents the Comanche Nation while H. W. Marschall, a descendent of John O. Meusebach, represents his forefather. Each year on the first Saturday in May, the Gillespie County Historical Society sponsors a day long tribute to the pioneers. Visitors are treated to reenactments of furniture making, quilting, weaving, knife making, and cooking. Courtesy of the Gillespie County Historical Society.

The Fredericksburg Knutsch Band plays into the night in Old Fredericksburg. From left to right are: Curtis Hahne, Gus Friedrich, Elgin Friedrich, Dick Streit, Heinrich Friedrich, and Edmund Friedrich. Courtesy of the *Standard*.

Top: One of the cultural traditions the settlers brought with them to Gillespie County was their love of music. Local composer and director Marc Hierholzer leads the Arion Maennerchor at a performance in 1994. The Maennerchor has been in existence since the early 1900s and continues to participate in the Saengerfest. Courtesy of the *Standard*.

Ruth Nettle demonstrates bread making with cooked cheese for visitors at the Founders Day celebration. Courtesy of the *Standard*.

This is a sketch of Guenther's mill drawn by Hermann Lungkwitz with his home in the background. Courtesy of the Pioneer Flour Mills.

Chapter Ten

Trade and Commerce

During the colony's first two years money was scarce and provisions even scarcer. Many settlers left the community and headed for the Guadalupe to make and sell shingles. Others went to San Antonio or Austin to find work. Perhaps the only one with a secure job was the man who drove the two-wheeled oxcart all day long back and forth between the town and the cemetery. The food supply was also limited, and until 1848, the settlers had yet to harvest even one crop of vegetables. The Comanche Indians assisted the colony by bringing them wild game and honey in deer skins.

The demise of the colony seemed imminent, but in 1848 U.S. soldiers came riding into the settlement bringing hard

This store was located on the corner of Main Street and Llano where the present day Old Bank Mall is now standing. The store was owned by F. W. Lochte and his brother-in-law Felix Reinbach. The store sold a variety of things including, as the sign indicates, brick cheese, sausage, and bread all at "low prices." Circa 1900, courtesy of Ken Crenwelge.

Jacob Kraus Soda Fabrik was established in 1892 at 427 West Main Street. Later the business became known as Fredericksburg Bottling Works. The Kraus family bottled soda water. The first flavors were strawberry "rotes" and lemon "weises." The first franchise flavor they bottled was Iron Brew and then later Coca Cola, Orange Crush, and other nationally known brands. The drinks were sold here in town and delivered to neighboring towns. Shown in the photo from left to right are: Mrs. Jacob Kraus holding infant son, Erwin C. Kraus, Jacob Kraus, and Albert McDougal. Courtesy of Trudy Kraus.

This photo was taken of Carl Hilmar Guenther, at twenty-five, on October 1, 1851, as he departed Germany for America. Once in Texas he purchased land on the Live Oak Creek and began his Live Oak Mill. His mill was successful, but he later determined he would do better by moving to San Antonio to build a larger mill. He did, and his company, Pioneer Flour Mills in San Antonio, is still in operation. Guenther was rather diligent in writing to his family in Germany. His letters were translated and compiled in 1952. This quote is from one of his letters written on September 8, 1856. It depicts business life in the growing city of Fredericksburg.

"We are both well, praise the Lord, and are living as happily and joyfully as anyone can; at the same time we keep moving forward. The mill grinds constantly. Within the last three years, three mills have been built in the surrounding countryside, but none of them can furnish much. All the wagons come direct to Live Oak Mill because the others can grind only a horse's load or a mule's load. This competition has cost me nothing; in fact, I have gained by it. One of these mills in is Fredericksburg. [A man] started it three years ago, i.e., in 1853. In 1854 his $3,000 were spent in building and drinking, and the mill was only half completed. Now he has nothing left and must work as a day laborer to earn his living . . . The other mill, twelve miles from here, was started by Altgelt, from Barmen. He is very wealthy, and his uncle in New York is a millionaire. Altgelt (20 years old) is agent for his uncle, who wants to found a city and and call it Comfort. He built a saw mill which cost him $10,000, but is being so badly run that it does not make expenses. One good operator could really make money there, for there is good wood in the vicinity. Two miles away there is a saw mill which is earning good money. You will see out of all this that it is here as in Germany. One prospers; the other is wiped out. But, on the average, things go faster here, and most of them stay on top." Courtesy of the Pioneer Flour Mills.

currency. The following year Forty-niners brought in more cash and finally the town was up and running. Soon the once doomed settlement began to thrive. Stores, blacksmith shops, and cabinet shops opened. In 1849 the real and personal property value in Gillespie County was $25,278. By 1860 it had risen to $470,240. One of the most successful businessmen was Frank van der Stucken. His success was a prototype of the American dream. Stucken first worked as a newspaper carrier, then as typesetter. He learned the retail business from Chester Starks and in less than five years he had a business of his own and was worth $40,000. Folks in town called him "little Frank" or "The Little Rothchild."

Other businesses also thrived at this time. "In 1860, Fredericksburg . . . reported ten cabinet shops large enough to be listed on the census of manufacture—more shops than any other city in Texas." (Taylor, p. 34) However, with the onset of the Civil War, the Germans again faced severe trials. Gillespie County was primarily comprised of individuals who had come to America with idealistic hopes for independence and freedom. For most the concept of slavery was incongruous with those two principles. Furthermore, they desired to remain a part of the Union. Several individuals spoke freely regarding their anathema for slavery as well as their loyalty toward the Union. Some of them paid dearly for their sentiments. Martial law came to the county and drastic means were taken to silence opposition to the Confederate cause. Men were often taken from their homes in the night and hung from a tree. Through this horrific political crisis the county pressed on. After the war was over the volatile feelings did not die easily. Penniger's fifty year book stated that speaking of these times "would merely inflame healing wounds . . . and renew old enmities." (p. 48)

Once peace was attained, the community again made

The Schaetter family has been in the funeral business for five generations. This is a rendition of one of the first horse-drawn hearses in the county which was purchased in 1885, three years after the business began. The family also purchased the first motorized hearse in 1918. Courtesy of Oliver Schaetter.

"Starches, Spices, Extracts and Baking Powder Are All Right," boasts Felix Reinbach circa 1910 in the Fair Parade. Today local businesses from around the county still advertise their goods and services in the County Fair Parade. Courtesy of Ken Crenwelge.

Richard Henke and his son Udo Henke stand in front of Henke Meat Market. The building which is still standing is located on Main Street and Lincoln next to the birthplace of Admiral Nimitz. Courtesy of RoShell Baker.

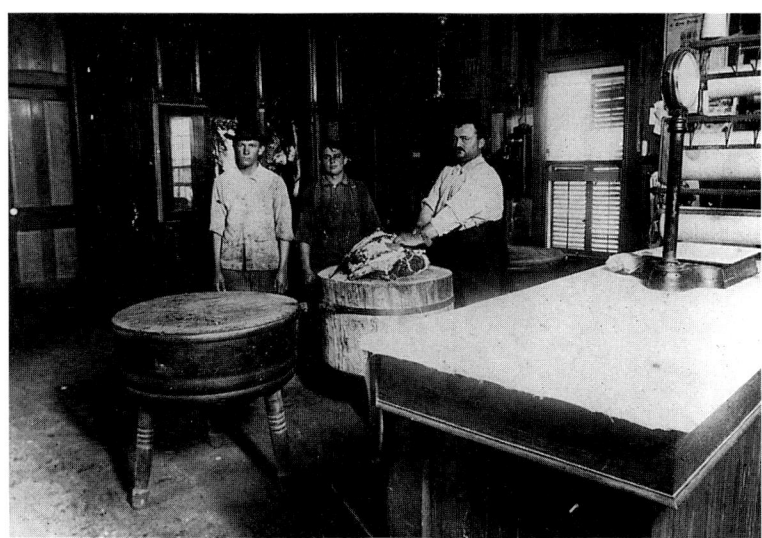

Richard Henke and employees cut up the meat for the day circa 1880. Courtesy of RoShell Baker.

economic progress. The Progressive Society was formed with the intent to improve the road system; one of their main projects included the long and difficult task of acquiring a railroad. At last in 1913, the Fredericksburg and Northern Railroad came to town. With this arrival came the development of small communities along the railway's path. Cain City was named for Charlie Cain, a San Antonio businessman who had helped make the railroad possible. Grapetown was also on the railway's path and the depot there was named Bankersmith after Temple Smith, a respected Fredericksburg banker. A company announced plans to build a large resort with seventy-five rooms and a golf course close to the railroad tunnel. It was hoped that Texans would make their summer home at the resort. Meanwhile, merchants and businessmen took advantage of the new railroad to ship cotton, commodities, livestock, and grain.

With the help of hardworking citizens, progress was making its way to the county. In 1920 the Chamber of Commerce was founded and in 1928 the town incorporated. Still various difficulties lay ahead. Ironically, in 1932 during the Great Depression both banks failed in Fredericksburg on the same day. Meanwhile, trouble was brewing in Germany. As Hitler's forces began overtaking Europe the general sentiment in Gillespie County was that the United States should remain neutral. Later, when the U.S. finally became involved in the worldwide clash, Gillespie County citizens were accused of being German sympathizers and speaking German in public was curtailed.

The citizens of Gillespie County traced their heritage back to Germany, but now they were Americans. One thousand men and women from Gillespie County left the safety of home to serve in WWII, thus proving their fealty to the United States. Interestingly, many of the soldiers were highly valuable to the military due to their command of the German language. The war made its mark everywhere. By 1942 the railroad that had held so much promise and hope for the community was sold

Emil Alberthal, William Thiele, unidentified, unidentified, Harry Alberthal, Henry Alberthal (owner), Otto Ketron, Alvin Alberthal, Otto Thiele, and Ben Alberthal all stop work at Henry Alberthal's blacksmith shop long enough for a photo. Circa 1910, courtesy of Mr. and Mrs. Wilke.

The Rolling Mills in Fredericksburg was located where Bethany Lutheran Church on Austin Street now stands. Courtesy of the *Standard*.

Robert Blum, Minna Zenner, Joe Molberg, Henry Molberg, and Gustave Hartmann pause for the camera outside of the Robert Blum Building circa 1913. This building is still used on Fredericksburg's Main Street. Courtesy of Fritz Metzger.

An unidentified shopper, Robert Blum, Minna Zenner, and Gustave Zenner inside the Robert Blum General Store Building circa 1920. Courtesy of Fritz Metzger.

for scrap and portions of the rails were shipped to Australia for the war effort. Peace was finally regained and the Allied forces emerged victorious. Fleet Admiral Chester Nimitz, born in Fredericksburg, became a national hero. Plans were made to return the steamboat facade to the Nimitz Hotel and dedicate its use to a Museum of the Pacific War. Efforts began in earnest to make the county prosper. Tourism seemed the logical avenue.

By the 1960s trade and traffic within the county picked up tremendously. The election of Lyndon Baines Johnson as president of the United States brought his birthplace, Stonewall, Texas, into the limelight, stirring even more interest in Gillespie County. Prior to this time it was almost unheard of for land to be sold to outsiders. Now, however, people from out of town were seeking and buying ranches. Businessman began to capitalize on the German aspect of Fredericksburg. New ventures adopted German names rather than English and interest grew in restoration of old edifices. Meanwhile, nationally held hotels, grocery stores, banks, and hotels joined the community.

The newcomers brought more money into the community, as well as the need for more services. New schools, a central hospital, and an airport were added features in the county. Eventually the police department provided twenty-four-hour protection. The 1970s and 1980s were extended periods of growth and development in the county. And by the 1990s the county seat, Fredericksburg, had become a tourist mecca serving as the commercial hub of the county.

Today Main Street of Fredericksburg bustles as tourists visit a host of unique attractions. Businesses that have been owned by the same family for generations serve alongside relatively new ventures. The town teems with successful businesses which have been featured in a variety of national magazines. In light of the fact that most of the Germans who arrived on the first wagon train in 1846 came to the new land for the express purpose of finding economic freedom, perhaps this success is not surprising.

This is an interior shot of C. L. Ransleben's Wagon and Carriage Manufacturer. The shop was located at 417 East Main Street in Fredericksburg, shown here at the turn of the century. Courtesy of the Langerhans Family.

Railroads brought many things one of which was new towns. This photo is the Bankersmith Post Office at the Grapetown stop on the Fredericksburg and Northern Railroad. It was named after Temple D. Smith, a prominent banker in Fredericksburg. Courtesy of Kurt Kallenberg.

Top: This shot was taken circa 1926 at the Fredericksburg Implement Company which was located in the Kott Building in the 200 block of East Main Street. Courtesy of Doris Eckert.

Another town to spring up on the Fredericksburg and Northern line was Cain City. At one point it had a grocery store and a bank along with the depot. The tracks ran between the building with the long roofs in the foreground. Courtesy of the *Standard*.

This interior shot of the Bank of Fredericksburg was taken in 1929, prior to the Great Depression. From left to right are: Adolf Gold (president), Ralph Gold, Alex Henke, Edgar "Pink" Crenwelge, an unidentified woman, and Lawrence Knopp. Courtesy of Ken Knopp.

The automobile has changed, but the concept of a showroom has varied little over the decades of the twentieth century. This is an interior shot of the showroom at Louis Kott and Company's Ford dealership in 1917. Kott became the first Fredericksburg Ford automobile dealer in 1912. Courtesy of Doris Eckert.

Fredericksburg's Main Street, the widest main street in Texas, was once named San Saba Street. This shot, taken in the early part of the twentieth century, reveals the hustle and bustle on Main Street prior to paved roads. On the far left stands the Maier and Son building and saloon. This is the corner of Main and South Adams or Highway 16 South. To the right of the Maier building in the background is the county courthouse which is now the Pioneer Memorial Library. Note the horses at the street's edge. Iron rings to tie horses are still on Main Street's sidewalks in some places. Also note the tents across the street from the courthouse. Tents are still used today for events such as Oktoberfest, the Fredericksburg Food and Wine Festival and Kristkindl Markt. Courtesy Mrs. Geraldine Dittmar.

Top left: Weinheimer and Son General Merchandise store in Stonewall was started by Alvin and Adolph Weinheimer in 1906. Circa 1928, courtesy of Bernice Weinheimer.

Middle: There's black gold in those hills or so some thought. This was an attempt at bringing the oil boom to Stonewall in the 1920s, but what really gushed in that area were the peaches. Courtesy of Bernice Weinheimer.

Burg Brothers General Merchandise Store in Stonewall circa 1922. The business was started in the early 1890s. Courtesy of Bernice Weinheimer.

Top Right: Henry David Kammlah with his first bike which had wooden rims on the wheels. Henry David worked for Henry Jenschke who had a shoe repair shop. For two dollars a week, Kammlah delivered shoes on his bicycle, circa 1921. Courtesy of Henry D. Kammlah.

Bottom left: KNAF, Fredericksburg's local radio station, was founded in 1947. In 1959 the station under the leadership of its owners (pictured), Norbert and Alene Fritz, increased its power and changed its frequency to 910 AM where it still broadcasts today. Alene Fritz was one of the first women in the nation to be on the radio. In 1971 the station started FM broadcasting at 101.1 FM under the KFAN banner. Since then the FM portion of the station has undergone transitions and now broadcasts at 107.9 FM, also under the KFAN banner. The Fritz's son, Jason, and his wife, Jan, now own and operate the station. Courtesy of KNAF.

Top left: This is a shot of Edward Krauskopf in the Krauskopf Brothers Fredericksburg business around 1930. Krauskopf Brothers is the oldest family-run John Deere dealer in Texas and second oldest family-run John Deere dealer worldwide. The firm was founded in 1846 by Engelbert Krauskopf who worked as a cabinetmaker and gun manufacturer before turning his business to farm implements. Engelbert's son, Oscar, brought the John Deere dealership into the family business in 1881. Courtesy of the Krauskopf Family.

Above right: This photo of the Ostrow Hotel was taken before the third story was destroyed by fire. Courtesy of Jeanette Klein.

Middle left: The Keidel Medical Clinic on Main Street was built in 1909 by Dr. Albert Keidel for his four sons. Medical offices were located upstairs for Dr. Victor Keidel and dental offices for Dr. Werner and Dr. Felix Keidel. On the ground floor Kurt Keidel operated a drug store. Courtesy of Mrs. J. Hardin Perry

Bottom left: The Keidel Memorial Hospital was remodeled to be a modern day hospital in 1937–1938. Edward Stein and Albert Keidel supervised the renovation. It served as a hospital until the opening of Hill Country Memorial Hospital, and is currently used as a family practice clinic owned by Dr. J. Hardin Perry. Courtesy of Mrs. J. Hardin Perry.

Local gasoline dealers discuss sales strategies with company representatives in the 1940s. From right are Milton Crenwelge, Oswald Crenwelge, and Ruben Crenwelge. Milton, a young boy at the time, learned the business and later became a car dealer in Fredericksburg and Kerrville. Courtesy of Ken Crenwelge.

Whitetail deer were not the only game hunted in Gillespie County. These men were able to round up a couple of bobcats with the help of their hounds. Courtesy of the *Standard*.

Hunting has greatly affected the economic planning and stability of Gillespie County. Hunters from around the state and the country converge on the ranches in this county. In the early days hunters would park their cars and trucks in the middle of Main Street while buying their supplies from stores like Knopp and Metzgers and Dooley's 5-10-25.

German bakeries have a tasty reputation worldwide and Fredericksburg is no exception. This shot was taken in 1965 of the interior of Dietz Bakery at 218 East Main Street. Pictured from left to right are: Sandra, Don, Willie Marie, Edgar, and Theo Dietz. Theo had been in the baking business since 1917. Courtesy of Dietz Bakery.

The Radio Post was started by William Dietel in 1922. Since its inception, Dietel's children were involved and carried on the business after his death. The paper was sold in 1978, but was bought back by the family in 1984. Later in 1984 the family decided once again to sell the paper to the Fredericksburg Publishing Company, owners of *The Fredericksburg Standard*. Fred Dietel is seated and his sister, Erna Dietel Heinen, is seated to the left on the desk. Courtesy of Fred Dietel.

Less than a decade after World War II ended, Fleet Admiral Chester Nimitz visited Fredericksburg. This photo captures a conversation Nimitz was having with locally respected businessman Walter McKay at the KNAF studio on May 17, 1952. Courtesy of KNAF.

Hill Country Memorial Hospital's Medical Staff in the early 1970s. In the front row from left to right are: Drs. Lorence Feller, J. Hardin Perry, Walton H. Springall, and Herbert Merz. In the second row are: Drs. Edward Stein, Kurt Poehlman, Charles Burg, Wilbur Crenwelge, and Dor Brown. Courtesy of Hill Country Memorial Hospital.

The original section of Hill Country Memorial Hospital was built in 1971 on land donated by Dr. and Mrs. J. Hardin Perry. Their donation set in motion a tradition of community support for the local hospital. Since then HCMH has seen tremendous growth in its medical staff and services, has expanded its physical plant to more that twice it original size, and has had sound financial stability. Today HCMH specializes in medical services that are unique to rural hospitals. The community funded the construction of the original building through donations and has also helped fund several of the expansions. Courtesy of the *Standard*.

Volume one, issue one of *The Fredericksburg Standard* was printed on September 7, 1907. Originally the paper was named *Gillespie County News*, but was changed in 1907 when O. W. Faubion purchased it from R. T. Gliddon. In 1914 Faubion sold it to the Fredericksburg Publishing Company which still owns the paper today. The paper's name was once again changed in 1984 when the publishing company purchased Fredericksburg's other newspaper, *The Radio Post*. The Fredericksburg Publishing Company also published a German language newspaper (which began in 1877), *Fredericksburg Wochenblatt*, until 1946. Pictured in this photo is Arthur H. Kowert, the *Standard's* publisher, at his trusty typewriter which he still uses. He joined the *Standard* in 1934 as the advertising manager after graduating from the University of Texas that same year. He later became the managing editor and eventually was named publisher of the paper and president of the publishing company. Courtesy of the *Standard*.

The redevelopment of Market Square in Fredericksburg was a project organized in the late 1980s and early 1990s with the purpose of remaking a central square, or plaza, for local citizens and special events. The plan called for building of new pavilions, planting arbors, and creating walkways with pavers donated by local citizens. By 1995 three pavilions, walkways, and other additions, including the transplanting of oaks trees from the local golf couse, were completed. Pictured from left to right at the ground breaking ceremonies in 1990 are: Glen Treibs (Gillespie County Historical Society president), Tim Crenwelge (city commissioner), J. Perry (city commissioner), Boyd Harper (mayor), Jack Maguire, and Jay Weinheimer (county judge). Courtesy of the *Standard*.

Bibliography

Biesele, Rudolph Leopold. *History of German Settlements in Texas, 1831–1861.* Austin: Press of Von Boeckmann-Jones Co., 1930; German-Texan Heritage Society, Ann Arbor Michigan: McNaughton & Gunn, 1964.

Edwards, Walter F. *Fredericksburg Guidebook.* Fredericksburg: Gargoyle Press, 1994.

Gillespie County Historical Society. *Pioneers in God's Hills, A History of Fredericksburg and Gillespie County People and Events.* 1960.

Gillespie County Historical Society. *Pioneers in God's Hills, Vol. II, A History of Fredericksburg and Gillespie County People and Events.* 1974.

Gillespie County School Histories. Fredericksburg: Dietel & Son Printing, 1983.

Gold, Ella Amanda. "The History of Education in Gillespie County." Master's thesis, University of Texas, 1945.

Heintzen, Frank W. "Fredericksburg, Texas, During the Civil War and Reconstruction" Master's thesis, St. Mary's University, 1944.

Holy Ghost Lutheran Church. Dedication booklet, 1949.

Howard, Etha Johannaber. "The Impact of Urban Development on Ethnic Identity in a Texas German-American Community." Ph.D. diss., Dedman College of Southern Methodist University, 1984.

Hurst, Regina Beckmann. *Translation of Diary and Letters of Carl Hilmar Guenther.* Self published, 1952.

King, Irene Marshall. *John O. Meusebach, German Colonizer in Texas.* Austin: University of Texas Press, 1967.

Lich, Glen E. *The German Texans.* San Antonio: The University of Texas Institute of Texan Cultures at San Antonio, 1981.

McGuire, James Patrick. *Hermann Lungkwitz, Romantic Landscapist on the Texas Frontier.* Austin: University of Texas Press, 1983.

Montgomery, Ruth. Mrs. LBJ. City: Holt, Rhinehart and Winston, 1964.

Newcomb, William W., Jr., with Mary S. Carnahan. *German Artist on the Texas, Friedrich Richard Petri.* Austin & London: University of Texas Press, 1978.

Penniger, Robert. *Fredericksburg, Texas . . . The First Fifty Years A Translation of Penniger's 50th Anniversary Festival Edition.* Fredericksburg: Fredericksburg Publishing Co., Inc., 1971.

Rosenberg, Marjorie von. *German Artists of Early Texas.* Austin: Eakin Press, 1982.

Schmidt, F. A. *Rails Through The Hill County.* Self published, 1973.

Taylor, Lonn and David B. Warren. *Texas Furniture, The Cabinetmakers and Their Work 1840–1880.* Austin: University of Texas Press, 1975.

Newspapers

The Fredericksburg Standard Radio Post. Various issues.

The Radio Post. Various issues.

Index

A
Adelsverein Society, 15, 16, 19
Adelsverein, 9, 11, 12, 14, 27, 29, 45, 67
Adenauer, Konrad, German Chancellor, 157
Ahrens, Harry, 97
Ahrens, Hugo, 36
Ahrens, Lina, 101
Ahrens, Tillie, 136
Albert Saloon, 94, 136
Albert, 94, 137
Alberthal, Alvin, 177
Alberthal, Ben, 177
Alberthal, Cornelia, Mrs., 38
Alberthal, Edmund, 122
Alberthal, Emil, 177
Alberthal, Harry, 177
Alberthal, Henry, 122, 177
Allison, William, 13
Altgelt, Esther, 10
Altgelt, Helen Marschall, 10
Althaus, Christian, Dr., 18
Apaches, 25
Arizola, Karen, 168
Arlt, August, 36

B
Baag, Friedrich, 130
Baag, Willie, 96
Baethge, Felix William, 95
Baethge, Ferdinand, 92, 96
Baethge, Hugo, 92
Baethge, Lena, 92
Baethge, Louise (Eckert), 92
Baethges, 92
Baiglsley, Elaine Wilke, 54
Balanced Rock, 105
Bandera, 18
Bank of Fredericksburg, 181
Bankersmith Post Office, 180
Bankersmith, 176
Bartholmae, Varnell, 39
Basse, Cora, 164
Basse, Fredericke Charlotte, 14
Basse, Hans, 36
Basse, Heinrich, S. Wilhelm, Reverend, 14, 29, 30, 31, 33, 47
Bauer, Martin, 136
Beckman, Ida, 109
Beckman, Miss, 109
Beckmann, Carol, 140
Beckmann, Henry, 84
Behrends, Christine, 54
Behrends, Eugene, 54
Benson, John, 155
Benson, Peggy, 155
Bethany Lutheran Church, 34, 39, 177
Bettina, 20, 21
Bexar County, 27
Bierschwale family, 53
Bierschwale, William, 53
Birk, Peter, 87
Blanchard's Vulcanizing Shop, 122
Blanco, 27
Blum Building, Robert, 178
Blum General Store Building, Robert, 178
Blum, Annie, 109
Blum, B., 19, 159
Blum, Robert, 162, 178
Blum, Robert, Mrs., 165
Boerne, 21
Bourgeois, 10
Bracher, F. A., Mrs., 34
Bracher, F. A., Reverend, 34, 129
Braeutigam, Henry W., 88, 100
Braeutigam, J. W., 13
Brandenburger, William, 127
Brauer Auto Supply, 116
Brauer, Gus, 116
Bremen, Germany, 10
Brodbeck, Albert, 97
Brodbeck, Jacob, 125, 132
Brookshire, Don, 142
Brown, Dor, Dr., 186
Brown, Nolan, 165
Buckhorn, 93
Burg Brothers General Merchandise Store, 182
Burg, Charles, Dr., 186
Burg, Werner, 136
Burg, Willie, 96
Burrer, Iris Fiedler, 54
Bush Gallery of the Pacific War, George, 155
Bush, Barbara, 155
Bush, George, Jr., 155
Bush, George, Sr., 155

C
Cain City, 130, 135, 176, 180
Cain, Charlie, 176
Carlshafen, 10, 15
Casino Club, 87, 99, 110
Castell, Count, 9
Castell, Texas, 20, 27
Cherry Mountain, 128
Cherry Springs, 16, 70, 95
cholera, 27, 31, 67
Civil War, 13, 21, 23, 50, 50, 54, 58, 65, 126, 126, 130, 133
College Hill, 128, 129
Comanches, 10, 19, 20, 22, 23, 24, 25, 173
Comfort, 21
Concho, 21
Coplen, Earl, 39
Coreth, Agnes, 10
cotton, 68, 69
Cox, May, 147
Crabapple School, 131
Crenwelge, Anna Gold, 68
Crenwelge, Authur, Mrs., 38
Crenwelge, Edgar "Pink," 181
Crenwelge, Hugo, 68
Crenwelge, Lynette, 104
Crenwelge, Milton, 184
Crenwelge, Oswald, 184
Crenwelge, Ruben, 184
Crenwelge, Tim 187
Crenwelge, Wilbur, Dr., 186
Crittenden, C.R., 39
Cross Mountain, 6, 31
Crouch, Hondo, 109

D
Dangers, Gottlieb Burchard, Reverend, 14, 33, 125
Daniel, Marvin, 39
David, Henry, 182
de Rozas, Lorenzo, 20, 22
DeGeller, E., Pastor, 32
Deike, Emil, 136
Delaware Indians, 19
Depression, 69
Detjen, Albert, Mrs., 109
Detjen, Emmie Patton, 164
Dietel, Fred, 185
Dietel, Louise, 147
Dietel, William, 162, 165, 185
Dietel, William, Jr., 103
Dietz Bakery, 185
Dietz, Don, 185
Dietz, Edgar, 185
Dietz, Marie, 185
Dietz, Sandra, 185
Dietz, Theo, 185
Dietz, Willie, 185
Dixon, Mr., 62
Doebbler, Emilie, Mrs., 38
Dolezal, Charles, 119
Dooley's 5-10-25, 184
Doss Springs, 70
Doss, 73, 74, 76, 130, 139
Doss, John E., 76
Doss, Thomas, 76
Doss/Cherry Spring, 60
drought, 69
Duecker, Alfred, 89
Durst, John, 31

E
Easter Fires, 159
Eastman, Seth, 30, 31, 44
Eberle, Anna, 79
Eberle, August, 79
Eberle, George, 79
Eberle, Lottie, 79
Eckert, Benno, 108
Eckert, Clara, 32
Eckert, James, 84
Eckert, Max, 32
Eckhardt, Reinhold, 119
Eckstein, Charlie, 101
Edwards, Walter, 169
Elephant Saloon, 116
Ellebracht, Eddie, 136
Ellebracht, Ruben, 136
Enchanted Rock, 107
Enderle, B. L., 70
Enderlin, Florine, 167
Engel's Store, 96
Engel, Walter, 96
Engel, Willie, 96
Estill, Julia, Miss, 124, 165
Evers, Charlie, 58, 72, 73
Evers, Sylvia, 104
Evers, Wanda, 58, 72

F

fachwerk, 30, 44, 48
Farmer's Grain, 82
Fassel House, 6
Feller, Alice, 32
Feller, Augusta, 32
Feller, Elbert, 168
Feller, Emilie, 32
Feller, Flourine, 147
Feller, Lorence, Dr., 103, 108, 186
Feller, Myrtle, 168
Feller, Nancy, 168
Feuge, C. W., 128, 162
Feuge, Cheryl, 104
Fiedler, Francis, 54
Fiedler, Lauren, 54
First Baptist Church, 39, 41
Fischer, Mr., 133
Fisher, Henry, 10, 11, 18
Fisher-Miller grant, 10, 11, 12, 19, 27
Fort Martin Scott, 13, 18, 21, 23, 27, 48, 67
Fort Mason, 13, 21
Founders Day, 170
4-H, 83
Frantzen, Alex, 108, 165, 169
Franz, Wesley, Mrs., 38
Fredericksburg 1993 Marching Band, 145
Fredericksburg and Northern Railroad, 122, 176, 180
Fredericksburg Bottling Works, 174
Fredericksburg Food and Wine Festival, 181
Fredericksburg Giants Baseball, 107
Fredericksburg High School Football team, 138
Fredericksburg Independent School District, 129
Fredericksburg Knutsch Band, 171
Fredericksburg Progressive League, 120
Fredericksburg Publishing Company, 186
Fredericksburg Radio Post, 104
Fredericksburg Standard Radio, 6
Fredericksburg Standard, The, 185
Fredericksburg Tourist Park, 103
Fredericksburg Wochenblatt, 186
Fredericksburg's Food and Wine Fest, 159
Freethinkers, 29
Friedrich, Edmund, 171
Friedrich, Elgin, 171
Friedrich, Gus, 171
Friedrich, Heinrich, 97, 171
Friedrich, Judy, 104
Fritz, Alene, 182, 182
Fritz, Norbert, 182

G

Galveston, 10, 14, 21
Garner, J. M., Reverend, 39
Gartrell, Harry, 164
Gellermann, Patricia, 69
Gerlach, Henry, Reverend, 162
German Immigration Society, 52
Giles, Alfred, 51, 53, 55, 138
Gillespie County Courthouse, 26
Gillespie County Fair, 66
Gillespie County Historical Society, 6, 31, 33, 43, 58, 64, 99, 110
Gillespie, Robert A., Captain, 27
Glatzle, I., Pastor, 34
Gliddon, R. T., 186
goats, 76
Gold, Adolf, 181
Gold, Alvina, 109
Gold, Anna, 109
Gold, August, 164
Gold, Ella, 140
Gold, Harvey, 89
Gold, Jacob, 134
Gold, Luana, 168
Gold, Marvin, 89

Gold, Peter, 134
Gold, Ralph, 181
Gold, Woodrow, 89
Grape Creek, 98
Grapetown, 130, 135, 176, 180
Grona, Lillian, 97
Grote, Henry F., 68
Guenther, Carl Hilmar, 17, 29, 174
Gulf of Mexico, 16

H

Haas, Herbert, 136
Haengerbande (hanging gang), 126
Hagen, L., 159
Hagen, Olga, 109
Hahne, Augusta, 36
Hahne, Curtis, 171
Hahne, Kermit, 136
Hanna, John Austin, 7
Harlan, Tom, 62
Harper Presbyterian Church, 43
Harper School, 146
Harper, 40, 43, 62, 74, 130, 168
Harper, Boyd, 187
Harper, Lyne Klingelhoefer Lewis, 64
Harper, Texas, 61
Hartmann, Clara, 69
Hartmann, Edward, 69, 71
Hartmann, Francis, 69
Hartmann, Gustave, 178
Hartmann, Joe, Mr., 86
Hartmann, Joe, Mrs., 86
Hartmann, Suzanne, 168
Hartwig, Louise, 130
Harvey, G., 151
Havorkannm, 96
Heep, Virginia, 167
Heimann, Elgin, 169
Heimann, Wesley, 89
Heinen, B. H., 39
Heinen, Erna Dietel, 104, 185
Heinen, Erna Dietel, Mrs., 169
Heinzelmann, Pastor, 34
Henke Meat Market, 118, 176
Henke, Alex, 181
Henke, Alfred, 32
Henke, Elisa, 1
Henke, Faye, 147
Henke, Hugo, 36
Henke, Louis, 36
Henke, Max, 36
Henke, Otto, 100
Henke, Richard, 118, 176
Henke, Sidney, Mayor, 169
Henke, Udo, 118, 176
Henke, Walter, Mrs., 38
Hermann, Pastor, 34
Hieorhoelzer Band, 162
Hierholzer, Marc, 171
Hill Country Memorial Hospital, 183, 186
Hirsch, Henry, 162
Hirsch, Henry, Judge, 165
Hirsch, Louis, 32
Hoeltzer Band, 101
Hoeltzer, William, 101
Hohmann, Otto, 39
Hohmann, Otto, Mrs., 39
Holy Ghost Lutheran Church, 28, 32, 34, 35,36, 38, 104, 108, 166
Houy, Henry, 165
Howe, G., Pastor, 36
Hunter, John M., 27
hunting Industry, 71, 100, 102

I

Immel, Herbert, 127
Indianola (Carlshafen), 16, 20, 134

J

James, John, 19
Jennings, Waylon, 109
Jenschke, Arthur, 94
Jenschke, Alois, 169
Jenschke, Anton, 114

Jenschke, Henry, 182
Johnson, Lady Bird, 35, 55, 123, 167
Johnson, Lyndon Baines, President, 35, 123, 136, 150, 156, 158, 178
Johnson, Sam E., 123
Jordan, Louis, Lieutenant, 151
Juenke, Alvin, 55
Juenke, Emil, 162
Juenke, Emma, 55
Jung family, 53
Junior Historians, 140

K

Kaffeemeuhle, 30
kaffeklatsch, 109
Kammlah House, 64
Kammlah, Henry David, 182
Kast, Anna, 32
Keidel Medical Clinic, The, 183
Keidel Memorial Hospital, The, 183
Keidel, Albert, Dr., 47, 48, 52, 183
Keidel, Felix, 57
Keidel, Felix, Dr., 105, 183
Keidel, Hattie, 57
Keidel, Kurt, 57, 183
Keidel, Margaret, 57
Keidel, Victor, Dr., 52, 77, 92, 159, 183
Keidel, Victor, Mrs., 165
Keidel, Wilhelm (William), Dr., 18, 27
Ketron, Otto, 177
KFAN, 182
Kiehne, Elise Henke, 109
Klaerner's Park, 96
Klaerners Opera House, 129
Kleck, Friederich, 32
Kleck, John, 57
Kleck, Manuela, 36
Klier, Alton, 127
Klier, William Friederich Eduard, 21
Klingelhoefer, Johann Jost, 54
Klingelhoefer, Robert W., 165, 169
Klinksiek, Arnold, Mrs., 38
Klinksiek, Belton, 169
KNAF, 92, 97, 182, 185
Kneese, A. H., 162
Knopp and Metzger, 167, 184
Knopp, Emma Weidenfeller, 52
Knopp, J. J., 48
Knopp, Lawrence, 181
Knopp, Willie, Jr., 52
Koch, Christian, 34
Koerner, A., Reverend, 162
Kolmeier, Otto, Mrs., 38
Koock, Guich, 109
Kordzik, Emil, 32, 162
Kordzik, Louis, Mrs., 38
Kordzik, Ottilie, 32
Kott, Charlie, 77
Kott, Charlie, Mrs., 77
Kott, Hilda, 101
Kott, Rudolf, 36
Kowert, Arthur H., 165, 169, 186
Kowert, Oliver, 89
Kramer, Meta, 36
Kramer, Minna, 36
Kraus Soda Fabrik, Jacob, 174
Kraus, Christian, 126, 134
Kraus, Erwin C., 174
Kraus, Jacob, 174
Kraus, Jacob, Mrs., 174
Krauskopf Brothers, 183
Krauskopf, Edward, 183
Krauskopf, Engelbert, 183
Krauskopf, Hermina, 104
Krauskopf, Lawrence, 162, 165
Krauskopf, Linda, 104
Kriewitz, Emil, 20, 21
Kristkindl Markt, 159, 181
Krueger, Jake, 100
Kuechler, Jacob, 21
Kuenemann, 50, 61, 118
Kuhlmann, Wilhelm, 36
Kunz, Kenneth, 82
Kunz, Max, 111

L

Lady Billies, 142
Lady Bird Johnson Park, 101
Lady Bird, 150
Landis, Peggy, 104
Lange's Mill, 74, 76
Lange, Craig, 168
Lange, Sarah, 168
LBJ Library, 123
LBJ Park, 149
Lehmann, Hermann, 25
Lehmann, Willie, 25
Leiningen, 20
Lentz, G. G. H., 13
Leonard, Edgar, 136
Lewis Ranch, 70, 99
Lewis, Jack C., 70
Lewis, John, 71
Lewis, William C., 70, 99
Leyendecker, Johann, 30, 39, 125, 132, 134
Liles, Larry, 170
Lindemannn School, 134
Lindenberg, O., Mrs., 38
Lingsweiler, Lula, 109
Live Oak Community, 18, 56
Live Oak Creek, 174
Live Oak Mill, 174
Llano, 27
Lochte, Adolf, 32
Lochte, Elsie, 142
Lochte, F. W., 173
Lochte, Friedrich "Fritz", 15
Lochte, Henry, Mrs., 165
Lochte, Mrs., 19
Loeffler-Weber home, 58
Loudon, Vicki, 104
Louis Kott and Company's Ford, 181
Loyal Valley, 9, 25
Luckenbach family, 95
Luckenbach, 96
Luckenbach, 98, 101, 109
Luckenbach, Elmer, 116
Luckenbach, Weston J., 116
Ludwig, Richard, 162
Lungkwitz, Adolph, 17, 22
Lungkwitz, Hermann, 17, 22

M

Maenius, Alvin, Jr., 94
Maenius, Alvin, Sr., 94
Maenius, George, 94
Maenius, Hugo, 94
Maennerchor, 171
Maguire, Jack, 187
Maier and Son, 181
Maier, E., 63
Maier, F. J., Mrs., 142
Maner, Friedrich, 32
Marie, Alma, 111
Marienkirche, 31, 36, 39, 40
Market Square, 187
Marktplatz, 62, 134
Marschall, H. W., 170
Marschall, Viola, 101
Martin, Joseph, 49
Masken Ball, 99, 110
Mason, 27
Mathisen, Fred, 169
Max, Adolf, 56
McDermott, Mr., 55
McDermott, Mrs., 55
McDougal, Albert, 174
McKavett, 21
McKay, Walter, 185
Meier, Ferdinand, 94
Meier, Martin, 127
Menzel, Father, 31
Merriwether, Mr., 70
Merz, Conrad, 19
Merz, Herbert, 186
Methodist Church, 33, 43, 128
Metzger, Adam, Mr., 86
Metzger, Adam, Mrs., 86
Metzger, Alfred C., 111

Metzger, Alla A., 111
Metzger, Bob, 167
Metzger, Fritz, 167
Metzger, John, Mr., 86
Metzger, John, Mrs., 86
Metzger, Oscar William, 36
Metzger, Peter, Mr., 86
Metzger, Peter, Mrs., 86
Metzger, Sidney Matthew, 36
Metzger, Tilda, 167
Meurer, Otto, 93
Meusebach Creek, 133
Meusebach, John O., 9, 10, 12, 14, 15, 16, 18, 19, 20, 22, 23, 27, 107, 170
Meusebach, Marschall, 10
Mexican Jacals, 45
Mexican-American War, 14
Moellering, Cora, 36
Moellering, Max, Mrs., 38
Molberg, Joe, Mayor, 165, 178
Molbert, Henry, 178
Mopechucope, Chief, 23
Mormon settlement, 68
Mormons, 48, 67
Morris Ranch School House, 138
Morris Ranch, 164
Morris, Jim , 62
Morris, R. H., 39
Moursund, Albert, 164
Mueller, Otto, 36
Mueller, Rudolph, 100
Mund, 60

N
Nebgen, Alois, 136
Neffendorf, Alfred, 165
Neighbors, Major, 23
Nettle, Ruth, 171
New Braunfels, 11, 12, 14, 15, 16, 20, 27, 45, 119
Ney, Elisabet, 42
Night in Old Fredericksburg, 159, 171
Nimitz Hotel, 27, 99, 110, 152, 153, 178
Nimitz Museum, 153
Nimitz, Charles Henry, 152
Nimitz, Chester W., Fleet Admiral, 149, 154, 157, 159, 178, 185
Nueces Massacre, 21

O
Ochs, H., 159
Ochs, Heinrich, 125, 133
Ochs, Hermann, 159
Oktoberfest, 159, 169, 181
Old Methodist Church, 6
Opera House and Peter's Hall, 106
Ostrow Hotel, 183
Otte, Felix, 36
Ottmers, Rubin, 136
Ottmers, Wallace, 169

P
Parker, Quanah, 25
Patton, Albert Lee, 65
Patton, L., 159
peach industry, 70, 71
Peach Jamboree, 168
peanuts, 69
Pedregon, Hector, 169
Pehl, Albert, 96
Pehl, John, 84
Pehl, Theodore, 96
Pehl, Walter, 98
Penniger, 68
Perry, J. Hardin, 52, 183, 186
Perry, J. Hardin, Mrs., 169
Perry, J. Hardin, Mrs., 186
Perry, J., 187
Peter's Bar, 106
Petermann, August, 32
Petmecky, William M., 169
Petmecky, William, 165

Petri, Richard, 21, 22, 23
Petsch, Genivieve, 167
Petsch, Kathleen, 167
Pfeil Blacksmith, 49
Pfeil Gin, The, 72
Pfeil, Felix, 72
Pfeil, Otto, 72
Pfiester, Adele, 79
Pfiester, Adolph, 79
Pfiester, Alfred, 72, 78, 79
Pfiester, Alma, 79
Pfiester, Benno, 78
Pfiester, Berthold, 36, 78
Pfiester, Berthold, Mrs., 38
Pfiester, Edward, 78
Pfiester, Erna, 36
Pfiester, Felix E., 72, 78, 79
Pfiester, Felix, Mrs., 79
Pfiester, Frida, 78
Pfiester, Lydia, 79
Pioneer Home, 6
Pioneer Memorial Library, 26, 51, 59, 63, 114
Pioneer Museum, 58
Pioneers in God's Hills, 6, 140
Pioneers in God's Hills, Vol II, 6
Pittman, Carol, 104
Plaza Hotel, 63
Poehlman, Kurt, Dr., 186
Priess, Alice, 36
Priess, Alma, 36
Priess, Carl, 34, 75
Priess, Charles, 52
Priess, Mrs., 34
Progressive Society, The, 176
PTA, 147

R
Radio Post, The, 185, 186
Ransleben's Wagon and Carriage Manufacturer, C. L., 179
Ransleben, Max, 36
Ransleben, Meta, 36
Real, Felix, 77
Rech, Norman, 169
Reinbach, Felix, 1, 100, 173
Reinbach, Max, 165
Rheingold, 18, 134
Rhythm Kings, 89
Riley, Crocket, 131
Riley, E. H., 105
Roach, Eldred, 168
Rocky Hill, 135
Roemer, Ferdinand, 23
Rolling Mills, 60, 177
Roos, Carl, 71
Roosevelt, Franklin Delano, 69
Rusche, Alfred, 92
Rusche, Minna Baethge, 92

S
Sagebiel, Victor H., Judge, 169
Salt Branch, 72, 73
San Antonio, 17
San Saba Street, 159, 181
San Saba, 21, 23
Santana, Chief, 27
Sauer Beckmann Homestead, 149
Sauer, Alfred, 73
Sauer, Emil Henry, 80, 149
Sauer, Gordon, 155
Sauer, Heinrich, 32
Sauer, Maggie, 155
Sauer, Victoria Vale, 149
Schandua House, 6
Schandua, Peter, 31, 39
Schaper, Dina, 101
Schmidt, Alfred, 162
Schmidt, Alfred, Mrs., 38
Schmidt, Ebbie, 164
Schmidt, Ebbie, Mrs., 109
Schmidt, Emily, 147
Schmidt, Eugene, Mrs., 38
Schmidt, Gerald, 169
Schmidt, Henry, 77

Schmidt, John, 19
Schmidtzinsky, Max, 111
Schnappauf, Rud., Mrs., 38
Schneider, Eduard, Pastor, 31, 33
Schneider, Jimmy, 89
Schneider, Max, 39
Schneider, William, Mrs., 38
Schnerr, Emma Elizabeth, 42
Schnerr, Frederick William, 42
Schubert, Dr., 27, 30
Schuch, Lorenz, 97
Schuetze, Louis, 126
Schulpruefung, 127
Schumacher, Friederich Wilhelm, 31
Schützenfest, 170
screw worm, 70
scurvy, 67
Security State Bank, 59, 63, 114
Seelig, Katie, Mrs., 38
Seelig, Wilhelm, 36
Shaw, Jim, Delaware Chief, 23
Shawnees, 20, 22
Siemering, August, 126
Sisterdale, 21, 126
Smith, Temple D., 120, 176, 180
Society, 14
Solms, Carl, Prince, 10, 11, 12
Southern Methodist Church, 129
Spechte, Mr., 68
Springall, Walton H., 186
St. Barnabas, 35
St. Mary's, 55, 126, 135
Staatsverband Convention, 120
Starlighter Band, 97
Stehling, Alma, 111
Stehling, Cecilia, 111
Stehling, Charlotte, 111
Stehling, Felix, 169
Stehling, Max C., 111
Stein Lumber Company, 61
Stein, Edward, Dr., 183, 186
Stein, Franz, 126
Stieler, Adolf, 66
Stonewall Peach Jamboree, 159
Stonewall, 81, 113, 123, 127, 130, 136, 182, 182
Straube House, 127
Streit, Dick, 171
Stroeher & Son, Inc., 114, 119
Stroeher, Edgar, 108, 114, 119
Stroeher, Edgar, Mrs., 38
Stucken, Ella, 109
Sunday house, 55
"Sunday Houses," 50

T
Tatsch, 50
Tatsch, Belton, 101
Tatsch, Douglas, 168
Tatsch, Edmund, 101
Tatsch, Emil, 101
Tatsch, Ferdinand, 101
Tatsch, Heinrich, 32
Tatsch, Johann Peter, 47, 49
Tatsch, Peter, 54, 101
Tatsch, Reinhold, 101
Tatsch, Sophia, 54
Thiele, 50
Thiele, Hulda, 54
Thiele, Norman, 97
Thiele, Otto, 177
Thiele, William, 54, 122, 177
Thomas, William C., 76
threshing, 75, 80, 85
Travis County, 27
Treibs, Glen, 187
turkey plant, 82
Turn Verein, 87

U
Upper Immigrant Road, 27
Usener, Herman, Judge, 162
Usener, Lona, 36
Usener, Sophie Marschall, 56

V
van der Stucken, Frank Valentin, 150, 175
Vereins Kirche, 6, 14, 18, 30, 31, 33, 34, 59, 62, 87, 125, 131, 159, 162, 165
Vetter, A. R., Reverend, 162
Vogel, Carolyn, 140
Vogel, George, 127
Volunteer Fire Department, 115
von Arnim, Bettina, 21

W
Wahrmund, Alma, 36
Wahrmund, E., 159
Wahrmund, Elmer, 55
Wahrmund, Emil, Mrs., 38
Wahrmund, Ernst, 55
Wahrmund, Ida, 55
Wahrmund, Jane, 55
Wahrmund, Leroy, 55
Wahrmund, Theresa, 32
Wallendorf, Paul, 136
Walter, Peter, 35
Walter, Vernell, 104
Walters, Minna, 35
Walters, Otelia, 104
Warner, Bert, 169
Watson, J. Luther, 39
Webb, Earline, 104
Weber Sunday House, 6
Weber, August, Mrs., 38
Weber, George, 96
Wehmeyer, Ruben, 127
Weinheimer and Son General Merchandise, 182
Weinheimer Hall, 127
Weinheimer, Adolph, 182
Weinheimer, Alvin H., 102, 113, 182
Weinheimer, Charlie, 84
Weinheimer, DeAnn, 168
Weinheimer, Jay, 187
Weinheimer, Tom, 136
Weirich, Max, 36
Welge homestead, Conrad, 70
Welge, Heinrich Frederick, 16
Welgehausen, Conrad, 131
Wells, Ollie, 147
Wendel Lorenz, 74
Wendel, John, 95
White Elephant Saloon, 57, 90
Wilke, Amalia, 98
Wilke, Cary, 54
Wilke, Friedrich, 98
Wilke, Mildred, 54
Williams Creek, 137
Willow City, 137
Woerner, Perry, 169
World War I, 122
World War II, 69, 88, 139
Wunderlich, Alma, 36
Wunderlich, Otto, 36

Z
Zenner, Gustave, 178
Zenner, Minna, 178
Zion Lutheran Church, 33, 34, 129
Zizelmann, Philip F., Reverend, 33

961728

976.4 MOH
Mohon, Monty, 1966-
Gillespie County : a view
of its past